# CONSCIENTIOUS EQUITY

# CONSCIENTIOUS EQUITY

## AN AMERICAN ENTREPRENEUR'S SOLUTIONS TO THE WORLD'S GREATEST PROBLEMS

Neal Asbury

palgrave
macmillan

First published in 2010 by
PALGRAVE MACMILLAN®
in the United States—a division of St. Martin's Press LLC,
175 Fifth Avenue, New York, NY 10010.

Where this book is distributed in the UK, Europe and the rest of the world,
this is by Palgrave Macmillan, a division of Macmillan Publishers Limited,
registered in England, company number 785998, of Houndmills,
Basingstoke, Hampshire RG21 6XS.

Palgrave Macmillan is the global academic imprint of the above companies
and has companies and representatives throughout the world.

Palgrave® and Macmillan® are registered trademarks in the United States,
the United Kingdom, Europe and other countries.

ISBN: 978–0–230–10892–9

Library of Congress Cataloging-in-Publication Data

Asbury, Neal.
    Conscientious equity : an American entrepreneur's solutions to the
world's greatest problems / by Neal Asbury.
        p. cm.
    Includes index.
    ISBN 978–0–230–10892–9
        1. International trade. 2. Free trade. 3. Competition, Unfair. 4. Social
justice. I. Title.
HF1379.A83 2010
382′.3—dc22                                                              2010020915

A catalogue record of the book is available from the British Library.

Design by Newgen Imaging Systems (P) Ltd., Chennai, India.

First edition: November 2010

10 9 8 7 6 5 4 3 2 1

Printed in the United States of America.

*I dedicate this book to the men and women I have had the good fortune to know as I traveled the world and who are presently or soon to be pursuing their entrepreneurial dreams. The progress and well-being of our planet is inextricably attached to their success. We must do whatever is in our power to encourage them as they venture into the unknown, learn to live outside their comfort zones, and conquer their fears.*

# CONTENTS

# ACKNOWLEDGMENTS

WRITING A BOOK IS ONE OF LIFE'S AMBITIONS for many of us. Since embarking on this project I have heard the dreams of several would-be authors about a book they have started and someday plan to finish. I can say after passing through the adventure of getting a book published that it takes much more than a vision and a blank piece of paper to fill with words. It requires people who believe in you. Without the people who believed in me this book would continue to be a dream instead of something you can now hold in your hand and hopefully your heart as well.

It was possible for me to pour out my heart and soul in these pages because I had the encouragement of others. Some I knew before my book publishing adventure began and some I came to know as *Conscientious Equity* unfolded. They have all been indispensable in the telling of my story. This simple acknowledgment is not anywhere near sufficient to tell them of the endless admiration and gratitude I feel toward them for the steadfast, sometimes critical, but always sincere advice they have abundantly and without compromise provided along the way.

I would first like to thank my collaborator Lou Aronica whose words and advice have turned *Conscientious Equity* into the work it is today. He was there at each step of the way and relentlessly pursued the most pure and correct presentation of the facts. He believed in the importance of my message. Through his talents this work flows eloquently as it tackles difficult concepts that so few people understand and that have profound impact on millions and millions of citizens around the world. Through many trying times Lou kept my confidence high, imploring me to plow ahead.

I would not have known Lou without first knowing the Literary Lion of New York and the World, Peter Miller. He is one amazing guy. I am humbled to know that Peter believes in me as an author. One of my life's greatest accomplishments is having Pete agree to represent me so capably in the literary world. He was my biggest cheerleader and never gave up. He taught me about the publishing world, platform building, and how to be a better person. I must also confess he tells a good joke! He is much more than my literary manager, he is a true friend.

I was blessed to have Lou and Peter at my side.

I would like to thank my editor, Laurie Harting, at Palgrave Macmillan. She has provided valuable advice and insight. She understands the entrepreneur and always told me what was on her mind; and I am glad she did. I would like to thank Melissa Giovagnoli Wilson, who securely pointed me in the right direction and got me on my way. She was always a kind and reassuring voice that every author needs to hear. Her advice I hold dear.

I could not survive without the in-house support of Tyler Helms and Frankie Mendez who keep me organized. With so many balls in the air it is a wonder what we have been able to accomplish. Dave Brimm handles my public relations and has been a confidante and great sounding board throughout this process. He was always there for me at a moment's notice.

My talk radio show, *Truth for America*, is an important mouthpiece for continuously telling and updating the story of Conscientious Equity. I would like to thank my good friend and co-host Rich Roffman as well as Andy Korge of Atlantic Radio Network for helping to get our message out each and every week.

And finally and most of all I want to thank my beautiful wife Elizabeth, who seems to get younger every day as I grow older, and my two dedicated daughters, Anjelica and Alyssa, who have been my joy and inspiration since the day they were born. They have gracefully put up with a husband and father that has dreamed his way through life.

# CONSCIENTIOUS EQUITY

# INTRODUCTION

I CALCULATED THE OTHER DAY that I've traveled more than four million miles over the course of my adult life—the equivalent of one hundred and sixty trips around the world or seventeen trips to the moon. As a global entrepreneur, I've worked with dirt farmers in the Philippines, state technocrats in China, princes in Saudi Arabia, African chiefs, Mexican oligarchs, and Colombian industrialists ever wary of guerrilla attack—and these people represent only some of the dozens of cultures I have encountered in the past three decades. In the course of my travels, I have learned that the world is a tremendously varied place. There are vast differences in how a Korean manufacturer, a Venezuelan shop owner, and an Indonesian gamelan musician get through the day. However, it has become equally clear to me that, underneath the cultural differences, there are considerable similarities in what all of us want in our lives: We all want a fair chance to make a decent living. We all want to live without oppression from power-hungry rulers. We all want freedom from those who would steal from us to benefit themselves. We all want clean water to drink, fresh air to breathe, and a planet that is healthy for the generations that follow us. In talking with mothers, fathers, sons, and daughters all over the world, I've found that these principles are as close to universal as anything can be.

It is through the combination of the people I have met and the business I have done around the globe that I came to a surprising and dramatic discovery: we have in our power the ability to create the conditions that all reasonable people desire. This power has nothing to do with imperialism or strong-arming any nation into sublimating its cultural identity. At its foundation lies the belief that, if given the opportunity to do business together fairly, the people of the world can make extraordinary strides and the notion that global commerce can do more to improve circumstances at home and abroad than any group of elected officials ever can.

Free enterprise and entrepreneurialism can be the driving force in creating the world that all good people want—a world where poverty is far less prevalent, where everyone can dream of doing something meaningful with his or her life, where corrupt rulers lose their iron-fisted hold, where all who want to work can find a job that offers decent wages and a sense of dignity, and where our environment is safe for our children's children's children. Where philosophers wax poetic and politicians spew rhetoric, I see solutions—very real, practical solutions—to our greatest social ills. These solutions derive from doing business around the world in a progressive new fashion that allows entrepreneurialism and the American spirit of reaching out into the unknown to generate a new kind of transaction and interaction, in which there will be many, many winners and the only losers will be the corrupt and despotic.

I call this kind of business "Conscientious Equity." It is *conscientious* because it is the right thing to do and *equity* because we all have ownership in doing the right thing. This way of conducting commerce is bold and unprecedented. It faces many roadblocks, which I will address as we go along. Yet it is also eminently doable. It requires us to think in new ways about how we conduct business with the rest of the world, but it fits neatly into a framework with which entrepreneurs are already comfortable.

At the center of this concept is a document that I've taken to calling a Conscientious Equity Accord. It takes the notion of Conscientious Equity and positions it as the driver of the most powerful tool for positive change that we can employ: global commerce.

We have so many social issues to address that they often seem overwhelming. Too many Americans are living below the subsistence level. Around the world, conditions are even more desperate, with nearly half of the planet's population trying to get by on less than two dollars a day. Far too many people here and abroad live every waking moment with the gnawing pangs of hunger. Corrupt government officials hoard money and force their people to live without opportunity. Workers toil in shameful conditions at heartbreakingly young ages. Our natural resources are desecrated, our human resources are pillaged, and our air and water are despoiled. The gulf between the haves and have-nots grows ever wider.

Conscientious Equity Accords can address every one of these issues, and many others, by setting the framework under which America does business with the world. We know this can happen because we have already seen it begin. In the past few years, we have signed free trade agreements with some of our trading partners. These agreements have attached principled conditions as terms under which nations can bring their products into the United States favorably. We have every reason to believe that we can expand these terms—in a comprehensive way that addresses the things most important to us and to good people everywhere—and that the countries with which we do business will continue to sign on the dotted line. We can believe this because we have something to offer that no one else on the planet can match: we have created the most voracious consumer market in the world.

Although China's population is more than four times that of the United States, the U.S. gross domestic product (GDP) is nearly double China's. The population of India is more than three-and-a-half times larger than the U.S. population, but our GDP is four-and-a-half times larger than India's. Simply put, the American economy is, dollar for dollar, the most active in the world, even when compared to countries with considerably larger populations. Our trading partners have an undying love affair with the American consumer. And well they should; the United States excels at many things, but America's talent at *purchasing things* is overwhelmingly greater than that of any other culture in existence. Just as foreign exporters know what it means to have unfettered access to our market, so do they understand how much losing that access would hurt them.

None of the nations with which we do business is willing to consider walking away from the American market. In many cases, doing so would topple that country's economy and government. Therefore, if we want to have a real impact on the world, while at the same time offering greater opportunities for American entrepreneurs than they have ever had before, we need to have the fortitude to announce to everyone who seeks to do business with the United States that we will only grant the most competitive status to those countries that agree to sign a Conscientious Equity Accord with us.

Our detractors will cite the large Asian economies as one of our greatest challenges. Having lived there for more than two decades, I can unequivocally state what Asian cultures respect most is enlightened leadership filled with wisdom, power, and strength that emanates from a clear vision. These Confucian paternalistic societies look up to resolute leadership. Conscientious Equity needs to be communicated clearly and resolutely to our trading partners, and we need to do this behind closed doors in a way that respects their culture, face, and dignity. They will see the wisdom of this new vision as long as our leaders stand firm and squarely on the side of all good people everywhere.

Every Conscientious Equity Accord would include the following provisions, customized to consider cultural and economic differences:

- strong labor rights guidelines to protect all workers, including labor organizers, and particularly children;
- powerful anti-corruption language to allow average citizens from all over the world the opportunity to benefit from their hard work and ingenuity without the threat of greedy officials stealing their livelihoods;
- stringent environmental protections that curtail the despoliation of the land for profit and the spewing of poisons into the air that carry on the wind beyond any national border;
- access to the country's markets for American exporters under the same rules and conditions that we grant to that nation's businesses;
- ironclad intellectual property safeguards to give the entrepreneurial and inventive the security of knowing that their creations will remain their own; and
- rules of law and supervision that make all of these provisions enforceable on a global scale.

I'll admit right now that my presentation of Conscientious Equity and Conscientious Equity Accords comes from a distinctly American perspective. I am, after all, an American entrepreneur, and I care deeply about the people in my country. But if I have American self-interest at heart, it is enlightened self-interest. Everyone gets to come along for this ride, except for those who would cheat their citizens or endanger the rest of us. If we don't do this, we will remain completely stuck in the sand; our competitors will move further ahead of us; and, five years from now, we'll be talking about the same ills and inequities, in the same polarized way. If we don't build new coalitions—both domestically and internationally—Americans will lose, and a huge portion of the rest of the world will lose as well.

Conscientious Equity is about righting a wide variety of wrongs. Sometimes, these are wrongs perpetrated on Americans by others, and sometimes the opposite is true. Sometimes we perpetrate these wrongs on ourselves. We occasionally do this through ignorance or greed, and occasionally we simply don't realize what we're doing. Over the course of this book, I will address each of these and propose reasoned solutions.

As you follow me through the coming pages, I think you'll see how pulling these solutions together snowballs and provides a kind of unstoppable momentum for getting things right. Along with American democracy and the Constitution, our economy is our greatest achievement. It is time to unlock its intrinsic power to change the world for the better. In the final chapter, I will show you the world that Conscientious Equity begets. It is a world much closer to our ideals, but it is not idealized in any way. It is a world we can bring about by making a small handful of significant but eminently doable changes.

And I think it is a world where you'll want to live.

## CHAPTER ONE

# FREE RUNS BOTH WAYS

HONG KONG HAS ALWAYS BEEN A CITY that raises my pulse rate. On my first visit, in 1980, I got an adrenaline rush before I even cleared customs at the now-closed Kai Tak International Airport. The final descent into the city required a sharp, banking turn that made it feel as though the tip of the airplane wing were going to rip the clotheslines off the balconies of the apartment buildings that soared several stories above the green, jagged mountains. We flew so close to those buildings that I could make out the silhouettes of residents playing mahjong at their kitchen tables. A few seconds later, the plane's wheels struck concrete, and our 747 jerked to an abrupt stop at the end of a runway built on reclaimed land that extended several hundred meters into Victoria Harbor.

I had arrived at the world's most unrestricted bastion of capitalism—a place that, ironically, bordered on one of the most closed societies on the planet.

Before Deng Xiaoping initiated China's economic reforms in 1982, one of the few opportunities to experience the People's Republic of China in any way was to climb a ridge in Hong Kong's New Territories. During my first trip, I did exactly that, fascinated by the opportunity to get even the tiniest glimpse of a culture so isolated it might as well have existed in a parallel universe. As I made my way up the rocky slope, I felt my sense of anticipation rising and my heart pounding. I'd been to many foreign countries, but at that time China was beyond foreign; it was alien.

When we reached the top of the ridge, I peered through the trees into the valley below. I saw border sentries of the People's Army wearing drab, olive green uniforms and caps with big red stars. Flapping in the wind was the Communist Chinese flag, an image that struck me as disproportionately ominous. In the distance, peasants dressed in baggy black pants and large straw hats toiled in neatly embanked rice paddies, while water buffalo pulled their ploughs through thick mud.

I hadn't only entered a parallel universe; I'd entered a time machine as well.

In 1984, I was a member of one of the first U.S. trade delegations to enter mainland China. Our hosts transported us around the country in Russian-made military aircraft and plotted our trip carefully; only a few Chinese cities were open to foreigners. Government minders accompanied us every step of the way—and they strictly forbade impromptu encounters with the local population. They even tapped our phones to make sure they could keep us fully in check. We used a special currency called the FEC (Foreign Exchange Certificate) and could only shop in state-owned stores that accepted this currency.

During a visit to the ancient Chinese capital, Xian, in Western China, we stayed at a partially finished hotel. Throughout the day and into the night, large crowds gathered outside the hotel gates. The local people had never seen Caucasians before. I'm sure that for them it was as much of a science fiction moment as my first view on that ridge had been for me. As we walked in and out of our hotel, onlookers gawked. Fathers hurriedly put their children on their shoulders so the kids could get a better look. This fascination reached an unhealthy stage when we visited a nearby pagoda. A large crowd closed in on us. They grabbed at our clothes and pulled at our hair. The army personnel assigned to monitor and protect us rushed us to our bus. We sped away, leaving the police to clear the masses from the streets.

One of the things that struck me most during that trip twenty-five years ago was the tens of thousands of bicycles on the streets. The few cars I encountered were the property of Communist Party officials and their guests. Every bicycle rider seemed to wear the same blank expression. Perhaps these people displayed emotion in their homes, but on the streets they blended seamlessly into a humorless mass. The uniform blue Mao suits they all wore completed the effect.

On that visit, I stood on the Bund in Shanghai and looked across the Huangpu River toward Pudong. At night, the landscape on the other shore was completely dark. Pudong was closed and locked down. The entire city was asleep.

Much has changed in China since then, as the world saw during the 2008 Beijing Olympics. Construction and modernization are happening at breathtaking speed. Standing today on the Bund and looking across the Huangpu, I am awed by the towering skyscrapers of Pudong. It is as though people somehow managed to build Manhattan in a couple of decades. Shanghai is no longer a sleepy, backward city.

This is an extraordinary accomplishment, and it is nearly impossible to avoid being impressed by what the Chinese have done in such a brief span. As I gazed across the river on my last visit, though, another thought came to mind. Staring at the gleaming buildings, pondering the enormous challenges I faced as an American exporter in this country, and considering the record-level trade imbalance caused by China's selling seven times as much to us as we sell to them, the first thought that came to my mind was, *Much of this progress has come at the expense of the American worker and taxpayer.*

One of the tenets of China's trade policy is its ability to manipulate its currency, with the effects of distorting world markets and erecting barriers to American exports. These unfair practices have put a drain on America's financial resources— corporate profits that American companies could reinvest in our own economy, creating jobs for our workers and, therefore, additional tax revenue for our government that could be used, for example, to reinvigorate the Gulf Coast and our inner cities, rebuild our failing infrastructure, and provide job opportunities for the poorest amongst us. We need nation building right here at home. We don't need our money building towers in Pudong.

China is hardly the only guilty party. Japan, India, and many other countries have used decades of unfair business advantages over the United States to develop subways, bullet trains, and gleaming modern metropolises while our interstates and bridges crumble, our cities decay, and our people struggle.

Our trade deficit—closing in on one trillion dollars—is costing us nearly six million good-paying American jobs (based on U.S. Department of Commerce numbers that suggest that we generate a job for each $135,000 of exports). Dollar for dollar, exports employ nearly five times more people than imports and pay seventeen percent higher wages, so our workforce suffers every day that this huge imbalance continues. A reduction of this deficit by even half would have a profound impact on the U.S. economy and could resuscitate foundering communities all over the country. Right now, though, with the American market essentially duty-free to most foreign exporters while we pay export tariffs of anywhere from the teens to more than seventy percent, the opportunity for dramatic reduction of the trade deficit is nearly nonexistent.

The only reasonable way to resolve this inequity is by changing the terms under which we do business with our most important trade partners. As you will come to see in this book, revising these terms with Conscientious Equity in mind will have an impact that stretches from Pudong to Peoria, and everywhere in between.

## THE MYTH OF FREE TRADE

Although this is a book about international commerce and the profound social impact we can create by carrying out such commerce in a new way, it isn't a book about "free trade." Writing a book about free trade is a bit like writing a book about unicorns. They are both lovely things to imagine but divorced from reality. The reason is simple: free trade rarely exists between nations, and it is unlikely that it will ever exist. The barriers posed by foreign governments, whether in the form of tariffs, currency manipulation, excessive bureaucracy, product certifications, market distortions, corruption, or (as is usually the case) some combination of all of these, make it impossible for a seller of a product in one country to easily market that product in another country. Therefore, although one hears the term "free trade" bandied about with great frequency, especially among global entrepreneurs, the concept is essentially a myth.

I do know of one laudable—and very real—example of free trade. It happens in a market that forbids tariffs of any kind for any product or service; where it is impossible for anyone to manipulate or devalue currency; where a strong ruling body monitors and regulates all commerce; and where strong, enforceable laws exist to control banking, environmental concerns, labor rights, safety standards, and copyright and patent protection.

This market, of course, is the market between the fifty United States. Across a landscape filled with three hundred million consumers, products and services travel freely without any hang-ups at the borders or artificial inflation of prices. The state of Alabama cannot impose trade conditions that are disadvantageous to an entrepreneur from Vermont. If the goods fill a consumer demand, they will sell. Free trade amongst the states has served our country extraordinarily well and has given us the most successful and most consistently stable economy in the world.

Therefore, while acknowledging that truly free trade will never be anything more than a fantasy, we need look no further than our own shores for a model of the kind of business relationships we should have in place with all of the nations with which we engage in commerce. Our interstate commerce laws identify virtually every issue that we need to address to level the playing field for American exporters and generate a healthier economy throughout the world (and attend, as well, to numerous other social issues, which I addressed in the introduction and will address at length throughout this book).

American lawmakers seem to be beginning to understand this necessity, at least in theory. They have been able to put in place something we call a free trade agreement (FTA) with a handful of other nations. FTAs codify commercial terms with each nation. They address (and, often, all but eliminate) tariffs; establish uniform rules of law; and establish enforceable guidelines regarding safety standards, environmental issues, and labor rights.

In other words, they are a good start. Let's look at them a little more closely.

Before 2000, we had only four FTAs. Today, we have seventeen, with others pending. Although FTAs with Australia, Israel, Honduras, and Singapore, to name a few, mark a positive step forward, it is only a small step. The cold fact is that we do not have FTAs with the countries that represent more than ninety percent of our trade deficit. Until we do, we cannot hope to have any chance of creating fair opportunities outside of our borders for American entrepreneurs, and we cannot hope to improve living conditions for so many people at home and around the world.

We have been surprisingly timid here as a nation. Not only is America not leading the way with regard to international commerce, it is stunningly far behind. As I write this, the European Union (EU) has twenty-eight FTAs in place, with several others in negotiation. China, which began trading with the world just two short decades ago, already has twenty-one (though these agreements address very little other than tariffs). Even Mexico, which was a high-tariff, restricted market only a little more than a decade ago, has concluded twice as many FTAs as the United States has.

## NAFTA AND THE DAWN OF THE AGE OF AMERICAN FTAS

A watershed moment occurred on January 1, 1994. On that day, the North American Free Trade Agreement (NAFTA) entered into force, eliminating tariffs on most goods originating in and between the United States, Canada, and Mexico. There was considerable opposition to the proposed agreement in all three countries, and two side agreements addressing environmental and labor regulations became essential to passing the agreement in Congress. Even today, NAFTA is a political football, with politicians and pundits railing about the fallacy of jobs leaving our borders.

In reality, NAFTA has proved to be a huge benefit to everyone involved. The numbers are irrefutable. Today, we have a trade surplus in manufactured goods with Mexico and Canada. By contrast, our deficit with China represents nearly seventy percent on less than half of the trade volume.

As an American global entrepreneur, I can say with certainty that NAFTA has been enormously successful in opening the Mexican market. Traveling to Mexico City in the early nineties, before NAFTA, I encountered a dark and dismal place. Although this was one of the largest cities in the world, emptiness prevailed in the thin, polluted air. Within a few moments of arrival in a country, I can determine whether it is open for business, and it was very clear to me that Mexico City was not vibrating with entrepreneurial energy. Mexico was in a thick cocoon woven by an oligarchy that limited wealth and the creation of wealth to a select few.

Before NAFTA, Mexico had very few importers of American products. In fact, many U.S. exporters had more distributors in tiny Puerto Rico than in Mexico. Duties were more than forty percent, and value added taxes compounded the problem, pricing American products out of the market. Meanwhile, the oligarchy stifled entrepreneurship. The leaders monopolized the banking system, keeping it free from foreign competition. Local banks collected deposits to finance and subsidize the projects and investments of their owners and rarely loaned money to those outside the ruling elite. Ordinary Mexicans saw their life savings disappear through the devaluation and depreciation of the Mexican peso. Members of the oligarchy increased their wealth by investing in monopolized industries or foreign assets, resulting in the sad, old story of the rich getting richer and the rest dying poor.

Mexico still has a long way to go. There is still a great deal of corruption in its government, far too many people live under miserable conditions, and drug warlords wield unconscionable power. However, NAFTA has had a huge positive impact. Each year, my company sponsors a gala dinner for our Mexican customers and friends at the Hacienda de los Morales in Mexico City, a beautiful old building, erected in the sixteenth century, with dark wood and terra cotta. The Hacienda de los Morales was part of the original land grant bequest to Hernan Cortez in 1526 by the king of Spain, and Spanish conquistadors intended it to be a silkworm enterprise to replace trade with volatile China. Nearly one hundred and fifty people attend this event now, and it is always a celebration. It is fascinating to witness how favorably the Mexicans respond to American businesses. Of the one hundred and thirty countries with which I do business, none is a more willing or enthusiastic customer than Mexico. Demand for American products and services has multiplied in the last decade and a half. To underscore this point, Mexico buys more American products than China and Japan combined.

In addition, far from causing a mass exodus of businesses from our country, the United States has added thirty million new jobs since the implementation of NAFTA. Meanwhile, the influence of the Mexican oligarchy has declined. The largest bank in Mexico now is the American Citigroup, which is very open to financing small business. The largest retailer in Mexico is Walmart, which has a policy of buying goods and services from Mexican small businesses and entrepreneurs.

This leads us to an equally important benefit of NAFTA—the creation of a new class of young, dynamic Mexican entrepreneurs who largely look to the United States for ideas and business partners. Not only are these business leaders charting a new economic course for their country, but they are also generating jobs and opportunities for their people. This, of course, helps both of our countries. Mexicans can find more good-paying jobs at home and are, therefore, less likely to come here illegally.

NAFTA charted a path toward the creation of FTAs with all of our major trading partners. The primary function of the agreement was to remove tariffs and other trade barriers between the three largest countries of North America. At the same time, it included regulations that extend far beyond tariffs, which is a strategy we have continued to build upon with our other FTAs.

For example, our pending FTA with South Korea, the eleventh-largest economy in the world, our seventh-largest trading partner, with which we currently have a thirteen-billion-dollar trade deficit, includes a wide range of considerations. It includes clear guidelines regarding labor rights, aimed at maintaining standards for safety and working conditions to make the life of the Korean laborer better. It includes important environmental protections. Most significant, from our perspective, it includes strong intellectual property and copyright protections. Illegal use of American intellectual property in many parts of Asia is a huge concern (we will discuss this problem and the high cost associated with it at length later in this book). Without the governing rules and stated penalties of free trade agreements, we have little hope of forestalling piracy.

Although it is obviously critical that we negotiate new terms of international commerce that benefit the American economy, these agreements are a win-win situation for both sides. Estimates suggest that the agreement with South Korea will add between seventeen and forty-three billion dollars to the American economy, translating to thousands of good-paying jobs. Meanwhile, estimates see an increase in South Korean exports to the United States of twelve percent in the first year. American beef, banned in South Korea over concerns about mad cow disease, will have a significant presence in Korean stores (before the ban, Korea was the third-largest importer of U.S. beef) at a much more reasonable price, as the forty percent tariff on beef phases out. At the same time, Korean trucks will be more affordable in the United States with the phase-out of the current twenty-five percent duty.

The upshot of this agreement—and I need to underscore here that it is still pending at the time of writing, because Congress is holding it in abeyance for political reasons—is that relations with South Korea will be stronger than ever. This has relevance for a number of reasons. One obvious reason is that we need strong alliances in Asia given China's economic power and North Korea's hair-trigger leadership. Another is that we owe it to the 54,246 Americans who lost their lives defending South Korea and the 28,500 American soldiers still stationed there to make sure that South Korea remains the free and vigorous society it has become in recent decades. Freedom to make a good living was one of the freedoms that our soldiers shed their blood to give to South Korea. With Seoul a scant thirty miles from the demilitarized zone with North Korea (on the other side of which stands a 1.2-million-man army led by a highly unstable ruler), we want economic might to offset military might. Furthermore, the U.S.-South Korea trade agreement would be a crowning achievement for the huge sacrifices that America has made on behalf of the Korean people. In a very real way, FTAs have been silently replacing military alliances as the cornerstone of diplomatic reliability and shared interests. Perhaps this was inevitable. With the United States standing as the only military superpower—a position that will continue for the conceivable future—the rest of the world needed to react to achieve some level of balance. Unfortunately, we have not adequately reacted to this reaction. This is not a case of American chauvinism or believing that we should dominate the world in all facets; rather, it is a matter of wanting the United States to avoid falling further behind in an arena much more complex than military dominance, which, in many ways, could be a greater threat to our national security.

I have noted that the EU leads the way in negotiating and closing FTAs. As the political and economic union of twenty-seven countries, the EU is a market of nearly five hundred million people, which makes it marginally larger than the combined markets covered by NAFTA. Formally established in 1993, with a dramatic expansion eastward in 2004, the EU has made it more difficult and costly for American exporters to sell their goods to EU member countries, and FTAs have made these countries consistently more competitive on the world stage. A dramatic example is the impact the EU has had on our trade relationship with Poland. Veiled for years behind the Iron Curtain, Poland was always more Western in spirit than most other Soviet satellites. Therefore, when the Cold War ended, it quickly welcomed external goods and services. For years, Poland provided a welcome market for American exports. When it became part of the EU, however, giving European manufacturers access to its market at zero tariffs and implementing European product standards, we once again found ourselves on the wrong side of a free trade agreement. As the Polish market expanded dramatically for European entrepreneurs, our business remained essentially flat.

The EU has made it a top priority to create the most favorable trade and investment climate for European companies in overseas markets. Once we signed NAFTA, EU trade representatives immediately flew to Mexico to offer a comprehensive agreement, which was signed in 2000. Several sweeping EU agreements are in the works, including one with the Mercosur countries (Argentina, Brazil, Paraguay, and Uruguay). The Euro-Mediterranean Partnership is a venture intended to draw the markets of North Africa and the Middle East closer to the EU and to limit U.S. influence and business opportunities there. The Cotonou Agreement between the EU and seventy-six APC (African, Pacific, and Caribbean) countries that were former colonies currently focuses on the eradication of poverty and on human rights improvements. The ultimate goal, though, is to conclude an economic partnership agreement (the

EU term for FTA) that would give European products a huge place in these markets as their economies emerge.

The Chinese are also actively building free-trade zones. The AFTA-China Trade Agreement joins ASEAN (the Association of South East Asian Nations, including Brunei, Burma, Cambodia, Indonesia, Laos, Malaysia, Philippines, Singapore, Thailand, and Vietnam)—a market of nearly five hundred million people—with China's 1.3 billion people to create a free-trade zone that comprises more than a quarter of the world's population. With tariffs gradually reducing to zero and the advantage of geographic proximity, China will draw ASEAN closer to its economic orbit. ASEAN has traditionally been a close business partner of the West—and we have offered these nations significant commercial considerations to protect them from Chinese influence—but this may be changing. In addition to its agreements already in place (significantly more than America has signed), China has been very aggressive in recruiting more free-trade partners.

The implications for America are obvious. If the EU and China are creating favorable environments for their exports while we sit on our hands, we will find ourselves at a huge disadvantage. This is perhaps the greatest risk to our national security since the Cold War ended.

## THE FINANCIAL IMPACT

Although it is difficult to quantify what new international commercial arrangements would do to our economy, one can certainly project their impact based on the performance of our standing FTAs. In 2003, when we signed our FTA with Chile, our trade deficit with that country stood at fifteen percent of the total trade we did with them. In 2008, we had a nineteen percent trade *surplus* with Chile—and we now do more than three times as much business with Chile annually than we did before the FTA was implemented. The balance of trade has tipped in our favor, but, because the United States and Chile are doing much more business together than ever before, the FTA has had a positive impact on both economies.

In 2004, we signed FTAs with Australia and Singapore, two countries with which we already had trade surpluses. In Australia's case, that surplus has risen from thirty-one percent to thirty-seven percent of total trade, and annual trade between the countries has increased by more than fifty-five percent. In Singapore's case, the surplus has rocketed from twelve percent to thirty percent of total trade, and annual trade between the countries has increased by more than thirty-five percent. Again, the surplus has grown for us, but business has boomed for all the countries involved.

In 2006, CAFTA, our FTA with the countries of Central America and the Dominican Republic, came on line. Already, our trade surplus with those countries has increased from three percent to fourteen percent of total trade, and annual trade between the United States and these nations has increased by more than twenty percent. At the end of 2005 and the beginning of 2006, we completed FTAs with Bahrain and Oman, two countries with which we had trade deficits at the time. We have gone from a deficit of five percent of total trade with Oman to a surplus of nine percent of total trade, and our annual trade business has increased by forty-six percent. We've also turned a fourteen percent deficit with Bahrain into an eighteen percent surplus, while increasing annual trade between our nations by thirteen percent.

Our trade deficit with Canada and Mexico has actually increased since the implementation of NAFTA, but this is the result of our increased purchases of oil from these nations. Without oil, we actually have a trade surplus with those two countries. Since 1994, our total annual trade with these countries has tripled.

Based on our current record with FTAs, we can only assume that comprehensive agreements with our largest trading partners would net similar results. This would have an overwhelming positive impact on our global trade deficit. Equally important, if our new FTAs perform similarly to our current FTAs, we would see dramatic increases in the sheer amount of business we do with these countries.

This means increased revenues for all of the nations involved. At home, this would mean more jobs and a higher tax base generating revenues to address some of our country's greatest needs. A higher tax *rate* actually lowers the government's working capital, whereas a higher tax *base* (more income to tax) increases working capital, even if the rate is lower. FTAs would provide the former in spades.

## TAKING A CLOSER LOOK AT TAXES

At various points in our history, our economy has slowed to the point where we have gone into an extended period of economic downturn. The most damaging of these and the one that lasted the longest was the Great Depression, although as I write this, we are in the midst of yet another particularly thorny economic situation. Invariably, government officials debate—and often act on, as was the case with the New Deal and with 2009's stimulus packages—the notion of spending our way out of the downturn. This kind of spending always involves an increase in taxes of some sort. Raising taxes is the worst possible solution to any financial crisis, because raising the tax rate drives industry to seek offshore tax havens, sending jobs and money out of our country.

Our tax rate is already substantially higher than it should be. Nearly half of our states, when combining federal and state income taxes, have tax rates higher than any industrialized country in the world. If Iowa, Pennsylvania, and Minnesota were countries, they would be the top three highest taxed on the planet. Massachusetts, Alaska, and New Jersey would be numbers four, five, and six. Twenty-four U.S. states have a combined corporate tax rate higher than Japan, which has the highest tax rate of any nation. Thirty-two U.S. states have a combined corporate tax rate higher than third-ranked Germany. Forty-six U.S. states have a combined corporate tax rate higher than fourth-ranked Canada. And all fifty U.S. states have a combined corporate tax rate higher than fifth-ranked France.

There's little question that we need to rewrite the tax code in this country. Whether it is through a system like FairTax that eliminates income taxes and generates tax revenue through higher sales and capital gains taxes or through a complete overhaul of the tax rates we apply at federal and state levels, we need to make profound changes if we hope to keep American businesses (and the jobs they create) on American shores. At the very least, we need to reduce the corporate tax rate, provide tax credits for research and development, allow accelerated depreciation on capital expenditures and acquisitions, and provide tax credits for new hires. Such changes would offer the kinds of incentives necessary to keep American businesses invested in growing the American economy.

At that same time, if we want to fund the programs necessary to improve conditions at home, we need to expand our tax base. We need to employ more Americans and raise the wages of those who already have jobs. Doing so would generate an enormous uptick in our tax revenues, even with the considerable necessary revisions to the tax code. And if you had to put your finger on the best way to expand America's tax base, it would start with reversing our eight hundred billion dollar trade deficit.

It is widely believed that market barriers, manipulations, and distortions cost the United States five hundred billion dollars annually. I personally believe it is much more. The corporate taxes paid on these lost sales, assuming a twelve percent pre-tax income and a forty percent federal-and-state-combined tax rate, would be twenty-four billion dollars per year.

That's just the beginning. Some five hundred billion dollars in manufacturing would employ roughly three-and-a-half million Americans. Let's assume these workers would make an average of thirty thousand dollars a year. That adds up to somewhere around one hundred billion dollars in salaries. If we assume a thirty-five percent federal and local personal income tax rate, this would generate another thirty-five billion dollars a year in taxes. It would also provide millions of additional people with healthcare, further reducing federal expenses.

In addition, this increase in manufacturing would require roughly three hundred and fifty billion dollars in material purchases and other operating expenditures from American vendors. These American vendors would pay corporate taxes on that additional income, and they would also need to employ millions more taxpayers to provide these materials and services.

All of this would add up to a massive amount of tax revenue that we could invest in our failing schools, our crumbling infrastructure, and our desperate need for renewable energy. This increased revenue does not require raising anyone's taxes. In fact, it allows us to comfortably lower taxes instead. And it comes as a direct result of the vigorous and enlightened pursuit of international commerce.

I believe it is irrefutable that free trade agreements with all of our trading partners—and especially with our biggest trading partners—would benefit everyone involved. (Later in this book, I'll address some of the common arguments against these agreements and show how little substance there is to the positions detractors hold.) As I said earlier in this chapter, I consider the FTAs we have been negotiating to be only a start. In my opinion, we can do so much better. I believe that we are the only nation on the planet that can craft a document that our partners around the world would be willing to sign and that can fold nearly all of the world's most important social needs into a commercial agreement. This is the Conscientious Equity Accord I described in the opening pages of this book.

Entering into accords of this sort would shake the foundations of global commerce in a way where the only losers would be those whom we have allowed to act despicably and irresponsibly for far too long. Analysis of our existing FTAs has shown us that these agreements improve business for all parties involved. Our Conscientious Equity Accords would start by improving business—and continue to create a better world.

## CHAPTER TWO

# A Ship That Sailed Long Ago

ANY DISCUSSION ABOUT CREATING CONSCIENTIOUS EQUITY in the world needs to begin by considering the circumstances we have created for America's entrepreneurs. As I discussed in the previous chapter and will reiterate throughout this book, America is the only nation that can lead the charge toward Conscientious Equity because our market is the most attractive one on the planet. It—not China, Japan, or the EU—forms the very foundation of international commerce.

Yet, right now, American entrepreneurs face a treacherous marketplace overseas, much of it resulting from their own country's policies. How did we put ourselves in this place?

We're going to step further back in time in a few pages, but let's start with June 5, 1947. On that date, Secretary of State George C. Marshall stood before the graduating class at Harvard University and delivered a speech whose words would resonate for decades and dictate the course of American entrepreneurialism to this very day. "In considering the requirements for the rehabilitation of Europe," Marshall said, "the physical loss of life, the visible destruction of cities, factories, mines, and railroads was correctly estimated but it has become obvious during recent months that this visible destruction was probably less serious than the dislocation of the entire fabric of the European economy." Later in the speech, he noted, "With foresight and a willingness on the part of our people to face up to the vast responsibility which history has clearly placed upon our country, the difficulties I have outlined can and will be overcome."

With these words, the European Aid Program, which people came to know as the Marshall Plan, began. Its rationale—most significantly to speed the postwar recovery of Europe and to stave off the incursion of Communism into that continent—was sturdy at the time. Its methods—largely to dramatically reduce tariffs on foreign imports to allow war-torn nations virtually free access to the rich American market without any reciprocal benefit to American exporters—were feasible at that juncture. The American postwar economy was booming, we were consuming as never before, and our export needs weren't a serious concern.

The European Aid Program and similar programs in Japan did a remarkable job of stimulating the European and Japanese economies. Had these plans run their course and eventually been replaced by trade policies more consistent with the conditions of an economically healthier Europe and Japan, they would have marked a laudatory stage in America's world leadership. Instead, Marshall Plan export economics set us on course toward trillion-dollar trade deficits.

By the late sixties, it was clear that our global competitiveness was in rapid decline. Japanese stereos, televisions, and motorcycles captured a considerable piece of the American market. German cars redefined the high end of luxury vehicles for American drivers. Products labeled "Made in Japan" and "Made in Taiwan" loaded the shelves of American stores. The economies we had striven so aggressively to reanimate had become hugely powerful. American families filled their homes with foreign goods, but American products had a far more limited profile on foreign shores. Rather than rethinking our trade policies, though, we took the Marshall Plan model further. We threw our markets open, practically duty-free, to nations in Asia, Africa, and Latin America while our exports faced tariffs so burdensome that American products were ridiculously expensive—and therefore not a realistic choice—for overseas consumers.

One example of the how such tariffs affected prices in foreign markets comes from China. I have nothing but the utmost respect for the Chinese people and culture. I have spent years working in Asia and see the Chinese as some of the most hardworking and entrepreneurial people in the world. I also know that, as consumers, they make every effort to find the best deals. If American products were available to them at fair prices, they would be great and loyal customers. Unfortunately, the tariffs, value added taxes, and other barriers imposed on our products by the Chinese government have virtually priced us out of the market.

We will discuss China at length elsewhere in this book. I'll provide the details there, but the bottom line is that, through a combination of tariffs, currency manipulation, and the multiplying effect of taxes placed on top of import duties, American products in China cost as much as seventy percent more than they should. The Chinese people won't pay for such a markup, and it's difficult to blame them. After all, it isn't as though they can buy our goods at Walmart prices. (Walmart, of course, features so many Chinese products in its stores because it can sell them cheaply, thanks to low-to-zero tariffs. In fact, if Walmart were a country, it would be China's eighth-largest trading partner, ahead of Germany and Russia.)

Marshall Plan economics had their place and time. Now, though, they've led to American policies regarding international commerce that are, quite frankly, anti-American. This comes at a considerable cost to American entrepreneurs and the workers they employ. Exports have a huge, positive impact on the American economy. As I have mentioned, our exports pay seventeen percent higher wages and dollar-for-dollar put five times as many people to work as our imports do. If we came anywhere close to balancing our trade deficit, it's likely that the only Americans who couldn't find a good-paying job would be those either physically unable or simply unwilling to do so. The positive effects on our economy— including a huge recalculation of our tax base and a tremendous cash influx that would allow us to do all of the things we need to do to improve conditions at home—would be historic. It would also, for the first time in decades, put us on the right track for our times.

## THE SWINGING PENDULUM OF AMERICAN TARIFFS

Among the factors that have kept the United States strong and relevant on the world stage for so long has been our country's ability to stay current. Our nation has consistently led or served a vital subsidiary role in science, culture, entertainment, business ingenuity, political ideas, and numerous other facets of international life. The outlier is our approach to trade policy. Ironically, international commerce policy has always played a fundamental role in the American union. In fact, the second statute enacted by the fledgling American federal government was what historians call the Hamilton Tariff.[1] The act, which became law on July 4, 1789, imposed a tax of between five and fifteen percent on goods imported into the United States "for the support of government, for the discharge of debts of the United States, and the encouragement and protection of manufactures."[2] Since the first American income tax was still more than eighty years away, this tariff provided the only source of revenue for the new government.

In addition, the act provided considerable protection for American industry. By making foreign goods more expensive, the tariff gave American manufacturers a competitive edge or, at the very least, an opportunity for equal footing. Such thinking was the brainchild of Alexander Hamilton, the first U.S. secretary of the treasury. Hamilton believed strongly in an America driven by technology and inventiveness. In his landmark *Report on Manufactures*, Hamilton states, "When a domestic manufacture has attained to perfection, and has engaged in the prosecution of it a competent number of persons, it invariably becomes cheaper. Being free from the heavy charges which attend the importation of foreign commodities, it can be afforded, and accordingly seldom or never fails to be sold cheaper, in process of time, than was the foreign article for which it is a substitute."[3]

Hamilton had some very vocal detractors, chief among them Thomas Jefferson, who believed that America should be an agrarian society. Jefferson captures this message in his *Notes on Virginia*: "Those who labor in the Earth are the chosen people of God, if He ever had a chosen people, whose breasts He has made His peculiar deposit for substantial and genuine virtue. It is the focus in which He keeps alive that sacred fire, which otherwise might escape from the face of the Earth."[4]

Jefferson opposed tariffs (though he eventually softened his position) because he felt that Americans should be open to buying manufactured goods from Europe. Freeing Americans from the need to make these things would allow them to stay close to the earth—according to Jefferson, the most sanctified place for Americans to be.

Thus began a debate that has remained at the forefront of American policy for the entire history of our country. One side counsels protectionism (at times, isolationism), inflating the cost of imported goods to allow American products primacy. The other side advocates throwing our borders open to imported goods, believing that this is best for the world economy and that Americans should have access to everything the world has to offer at the best possible prices. Neither of these positions has served us particularly well in the past. As we move forward, both positions pose considerable barriers to our achieving Conscientious Equity.

The arguments posed by these polar positions have affected American entrepreneurialism in pendulum-like fashion throughout its history. The strategy of the Hamilton Tariff gained momentum as America industrialized, culminating in the Tariff of 1828, derisively known as the Tariff of Abominations.[5] The scale of the tariffs—which averaged fifty percent—catalyzed a seismic divide between the industrial North, which sought a way to insure the market primacy of its products in America against attractively low-priced European goods, and the agrarian South, which believed that European products were superior, needed the value they offered to build its own businesses, appreciated the luxury and comfort these products brought to their lives (as opposed to the hugely inferior and more expensive products coming from the North), and feared that foreign governments' retaliatory measures against high tariffs would close off foreign markets for its agricultural products. Some states unsuccessfully sought to nullify the tariffs, and South Carolina even threatened secession before the Tariff of 1832 lowered the average to a still high, but more acceptable, twenty percent.

The issue of tariffs that separated the North and the South was at least as divisive as the issue of slavery. In fact, although history remembers the Civil War as a battle over slavery, the issue of tariffs drove Southern secession just as much, if not more. In his book *When in the Course of Human Events*, Charles Adams shows how tariffs had a grossly disproportionate impact on the South.[6] According to Adams, nearly eighty-five percent of the income derived from tariffs in the 1830s and 1840s came from Southern imports, yet most of this money went to fund operations in the North. This ultimately led the South to seek independence. As soon as it did so, the remaining states in the Union pushed their agenda even harder, instituting the heavy Morrill Tariff.

After the Civil War, tariffs continued to be high, and the subject remained a political football. This led to the regular raising and lowering of tariffs through the first few decades of the twentieth century.

## THE ONE PIECE OF LEGISLATION
## RESPONSIBLE FOR ALL THE WORLD'S ILLS

Then, the stock market crashed. President Hoover had been elected in 1928 on a platform that included his willingness to protect American farmers and manufacturers from foreign competition. Many members of his party were elected to Congress at the same time for the same reason. The party platform stated,

> There are certain industries which cannot now successfully com-
> pete with foreign producers because of lower foreign wages and a
> lower cost of living abroad, and we pledge the next Republican
> Congress to an examination and where necessary a revision of
> these schedules to the end that American labor in the industries
> may again command the home market, may maintain its standard

of living, and may count upon steady employment in its accustomed field.

The new Congress made an across-the-board increase in tariffs one of its first and highest priorities. When the stock market tumbled, the strongly Republican Congress pushed through the Smoot-Hawley Tariff Act, the creation of Senator Reed Smoot and Representative Willis Hawley, both Republicans.[7] The act, which raised duties to more than seventy percent on some products, is one of the most notorious pieces of legislation ever passed in America. Although more than a thousand economists petitioned President Hoover to veto the bill, he signed it into law. It is widely believed that America's withdrawal from the world market (which Smoot-Hawley triggered) put the "Great" into the "Great Depression." The act turned a severe but manageable recession into a generation-long economic downturn that only a horrific world war could cure.

To be fair, the demonization of Smoot-Hawley is somewhat out of proportion. The stock market crash occurred eight months before Smoot-Hawley became law. At the time, international commerce accounted for just nine percent of our GNP. It is hardly possible that increased tariffs could have been the source of a forty-six percent contraction of the U.S. economy, twenty-five percent unemployment, and an eighty-five percent decline in stock values. When Franklin D. Roosevelt came into office (interestingly, in the midst of a financial crisis and on the heels of a terribly unpopular Republican president—this should sound familiar to anyone living in the world now), he extended our policy of isolationism and added layers of social welfare, unionism, and wealth redistribution that stalled economic recovery (again, sound familiar?).

Although the tariff's overall impact may have been exaggerated, there are indications that the extreme level of the duties imposed by

Smoot-Hawley led other countries to retaliate. American exports plummeted during the years it was in force. Because these were also the years of the Depression, however, it is difficult to know how much of that decline to attribute to tariffs.

Roosevelt did ultimately lower tariffs on a reciprocal basis with many of our trading partners. The issue lost luster, however, as the Depression and the growing troubles in Europe that would lead us to world war took center stage.

The next time tariffs became a major issue in this country was after World War II. The Marshall Plan marked a complete reversal of our trade policies. For most of our history, tariffs had been sizeable, if not onerous. Suddenly, we threw our market wide open, even though many of our most significant trading partners did not reciprocate. Without doubt, the Marshall Plan helped revive Germany. By the beginning of the sixties, however, it had clearly outlived its usefulness. Questions began to arise about changing our trade policy once again—not returning to high tariffs, but turning toward something that would acknowledge the presence of many robust economies throughout the world and the need for America to have equal access to their markets.

## CAPITALISM, FREEDOM, ... AND ONE HUGE OVERSIGHT

Milton Friedman had a different idea. In the mid-seventies, Friedman would win the the Sveriges Riksbank Prize in Economic Sciences in Memory of Alfred Nobel. However, it was his 1962 book *Capitalism and Freedom* that had the most profound impact on the way Americans did business with the world. By the time the book came out, America had racked up considerable trade deficits, causing consternation in many circles. Friedman used the following illustration to make his point that trade deficits are inconsequential and even a cunning prank by America at the expense of our naive trading partners:

> Suppose for simplicity that Japan and the U.S. are the only two countries involved in trade and that at some exchange rate, say 1,000 yen to the dollar, the Japanese could produce every single item capable of entering into foreign trade more cheaply than the U.S. At that exchange rate the Japanese could sell much to us, we, nothing to them. Suppose we pay them in paper dollars.
>
> What would the Japanese exporters do with the dollars? They cannot eat them, wear them, or live in them. If they are willing simply to hold them, then the printing industry—printing the dollar bills—would be a magnificent export industry. Its output would enable us all to have the good things of life provided nearly free by the Japanese.[8]

Economists championed Friedman's logic, and politicians embraced his recommendation that we stay the course in our international business dealings. They believed that our trade deficit was nothing to worry about and that the deficit was, in fact, a great benefit to us.

Friedman based his assumption on exports and imports balancing as the dollar-yen exchange rate, influenced by the invisible hand of market forces, would adjust to, say, five hundred yen to the dollar because of the oversupply of dollars held by the Japanese. This would price American products competitively in the Japanese market, reabsorbing all the dollars we sent to Japan to purchase cars, cameras, and consumer electronics.

However, Friedman made one crucial mistake in his hypothesis: he didn't anticipate that Japan (and, later, China) would purchase excess dollars at manipulated rates favoring their exporters while they constructed insurmountable barriers to prevent American products from entering their markets. In the years that have passed since Friedman published *Capitalism and Freedom*, instead of purchasing American exports with their excess dollars, these countries have been buying large quantities of U.S. Treasury bills, thus acquiring enormous influence over American financial and political policy.

In the seventies, the dollar teetered so badly that foreign governments began to sell back America's paper currency in exchange for the gold that backed it. Because we didn't have nearly enough gold to back every dollar printed and this run on our gold posed a severe threat to our economy, President Nixon made the astonishing decision to take the country off the gold standard. By 1970, we were printing U.S. dollars like comic books to send overseas to cover our expanding trade deficit. The gold coverage of the U.S. dollar shrank from fifty-five percent to twenty percent. Our trading partners began demanding "promise to pay" gold bullion in exchange for our debased paper dollars. Switzerland, and then France demanded and received their gold.

Nixon's worst nightmare was Fort Knox being emptied to pay for Japanese stereos and Taiwanese knickknacks. On August 15, in a televised speech carefully scheduled around the popular television series "Bonanza," the president used the lead-in to the show to ensure the greatest audience for his words. Instead of Little Joe and Hoss, viewers witnessed Nixon closing the "gold window," making U.S. paper dollars nonconvertible to gold. This was the genesis of the floating and volatile exchange rates we have today. It was also the beginning of runaway budgets and trade deficits fueled by paper currency that was no longer a hard asset, but rather a piece of paper that could be printed at will, the value of which was fictitious. Nixon's decision, known today as the Nixon Shock, temporarily buoyed the American economy. However, by debasing our currency and allowing us to continue to run up our debts, it led directly to the erosion of the average American's standard of living.

This attempt to gain an economic bounce by changing the underpinnings of our dollar should have strangely familiar echoes. If our printing presses ever landed in the hands of the wrong people, incalculable harm could be done. Take a moment to reflect on the developing countries over the past twenty years that have debased their currencies through deficit spending. Argentina, Brazil, Egypt, Indonesia, the Philippines, Russia, Venezuela … the list goes on and on. I have witnessed it repeatedly. Citizens work their entire lives and save what they can. Over time, they accumulate enough to retire. They look forward to some years of tranquility. Then, some corrupt, greedy leader turns on the printing presses, and these citizens' savings are devalued to the point where they spend their retirement struggling for survival.

That couldn't happen here, right?

Amazingly Friedman's influence continued after the Nixon Shock. When Japan swept into dominance in consumer electronics in the 1980s, the American government, adhering to Friedman's advice, remained calm and unresponsive. Based on Freidman's logic, if Japan was willing to subsidize its exports, American consumers should welcome such a subsidy gladly. Of course, things didn't turn out quite the way Friedman imagined. The Japanese "termite strategy" worked brilliantly by decimating, then eliminating, entire American industries. One wonders how many people at GM, for instance, are Friedmanists now.

Lenin once said that the most effective way to destroy a society is to destroy its money. The unrestrained printing of paper money to pay for our trade deficits (because we no longer base money on any tangible thing such as gold) has had a severe impact on American wage earners. It is with this paper money that we send our kids to school and pay for our elderly parents' health care. It determines where we live and whether we go away for vacation. Deficits debase our currency and drag down our standard of living.

Forty years of Friedman-inspired deficits have resulted in average real wages today remaining substantially below the levels of the

early 1970s. Despite the rise in the number of two-income households, median after-inflation family income has dropped. Evidence
of lower incomes and living standards is particularly pronounced
among younger workers, who are experiencing restricted opportunities for jobs, advancement, and income growth.

Milton Friedman believed that we should not require reciprocal trade concessions. "We should say to the rest of the world,"
he noted, "We believe in freedom and intend to practice it. No
one can force you to be free. That is your business.... Our market
is open to you. Sell here what you can. Use the proceeds to buy
what you wish." He cited Britain in the nineteenth century, at the
height of its empire, as an inspirational model. Britain embraced
unilateral free trade and opened its markets to the world without any reciprocal consideration for its industries. It is curious that
Friedman held up Britain as an example, because, as he could have
observed, within seventy years of this charitable gesture, that country was broke and beaten.

Our Friedmanist international commerce policies over the past
forty years have eroded American incomes and made our nation
susceptible to undue foreign influence. Friedman didn't anticipate
years of deficits, resulting in the massive accumulation of American
debt by the Japanese, the Chinese, and many of our other trade
partners. Yet that is precisely what happened. It is no coincidence
that the point when American's real incomes began their decline
was the same point when we devalued our currency and our trade
deficit began to grow dramatically. Meanwhile, we fear that the
Chinese and the Japanese could hold us hostage at their whim
because they carry such large amounts of American debt. Many
economists now believe that we cannot afford to get tough with
China, regardless of the inequities in their trade practices and their
innumerable human rights violations, because, if they ever called
in our debts, it would drive interest rates through the roof—a
doomsday scenario for the American economy.

## STOPPING THE PENDULUM FOREVER

The world has changed in countless ways since Friedman published *Capitalism and Freedom* and even more since George Marshall announced the European Aid Program. In many ways, America today is incomparable to the America of Reed Smoot, Alexander Hamilton, and the framers of the Treaty of Abominations. Therefore, our trade policy needs to accommodate the world in which we live, rather than the world we knew or the world we'd like to imagine.

Certainly, it isn't wise for us to send American tariffs into the stratosphere again. At the same time, in a world as competitive as ours is now, it makes no sense to allow foreign exporters free access to our market without having reciprocal access to theirs. Our total exports of goods and services in 2007 totaled $1.6 trillion. It is widely believed that not having access to foreign markets costs the United States five hundred billion dollars annually. I personally believe it is much more. The time for American magnanimity with regard to global commerce has long passed. The only realistic policy now and into the conceivable future is for us to work toward restructuring the way we do business with the world.

The path to such restructuring is Conscientious Equity. We need to enact Conscientious Equity Accords with every nation with which we trade. We especially need to make agreements with the world's most corrupt, manipulative, and environmentally irresponsible governments, because those on both sides of the agreements have the most to gain from them. Interestingly, implementing Conscientious Equity Accords with these particular governments would have a huge positive impact on our trade deficit.

In America, those benefiting most would be legions of small and medium-sized businesses (SMBs), the tens of millions of citizens they employ, and the millions more they could employ if we had these accords in place with our largest trading partners. SMBs have always done the heavy lifting for the American economy. They provide jobs for more than fifty percent of private sector employees and make up ninety-seven percent of all exporters. They produce thirteen times more patents per employee than large firms do. Over the last decade, SMBs have accounted for more than seventy percent of new American jobs. SMBs can move quickly to innovate and generate new forms of wealth creation. SMBs are, quite simply, the backbone of our economy. As we look at Conscientious Equity as a way to lift as many people in the world as possible, we must also use it as a way to support the entrepreneurs that have kept this country's commercial engine running. I hope you'll excuse me for repeating myself, but it is impossible to make this point too often: in the world of Conscientious Equity, everyone wins if America wins.

It is time to stop the trade pendulum that has been swinging since the founding of this nation. It is time to make the permanent decision to acknowledge that the American economy depends on access to all of the markets of the world. After all, ninety-five percent of the world's population and seventy-five percent of the world's wealth resides outside of America. We can't protect ourselves with protectionist tariffs, and we can't afford to maintain the deficits that our open-market policies have generated. The only policy that can sustain us is the policy I am so strongly advocating in this book: the policy of pursuing rock-solid Conscientious Equity Accords with every nation that wishes to do business with us.

If Alexander Hamilton were alive today, I think this is something even he would endorse.

CHAPTER THREE

# TAKING BACK THE KEYS TO THE BUS

In November 1999, the member nations of the World Trade Organization (WTO) met in Seattle, Washington, for their Third Ministerial Conference. The meeting drew an estimated one hundred thousand additional people in the pouring rain—none of whom was there to wish the participants good luck. They were there to protest the aims of the WTO. Their complaints ranged from the organization's positions on human rights, labor rights, and the environment to the influence of megacorporations on the organization's policies.

The protests started out vehement but orderly. However, they soon descended into violence and looting. As the Seattle police and the National Guard tried to keep order, they used tear gas and rubber bullets on American citizens, and a state of emergency in was declared in the city.[1] Such chaos on American streets—a rarity since the days of Rodney King—seared the memories of the citizens of the beautiful Pacific Northwest city. Many vividly remember where they were when these events unfolded. The protests and response even led to a feature film, *Battle in Seattle*, starring Charlize Theron and Woody Harrelson. Its scenes were so surreal that they seem to come from the imagination of a Hollywood action director, rather than the annals of our recent history.

How could something like a meeting of the WTO inspire such intense passion? Why were so many diverse groups so opposed to the works of the WTO that they felt the need to scream out their fury in the midst of a deluge? Why were they willing to run the risk of turning a great American town into a riot zone? The answers lie in the history and charter of the organization.

## GATT AND THE FORMATION OF THE WTO

In the aftermath of World War II, economies around the world were in trouble (although the American economy was booming). A proposal to launch an International Trade Organization (ITO) led to intense negotiations, but no resolution. At the same time, successful negotiations took place for an international tariff reduction treaty, the General Agreement on Tariffs and Trade (GATT).[2] Eventually, nations around the globe gave up the idea of forming an ITO, leaving GATT as the ruling international trade agreement. Signed by twenty-three countries, GATT had a direct impact on half of world trade at the time of its implementation. The core principal behind GATT was the notion of "most favored nations," which meant that GATT required all GATT member countries to treat each other equally and to treat all corporations from member countries equally.

GATT went through eight rounds of revision between 1947 and 1993 and ultimately had one hundred and twenty-three member countries. The final round of revision led to the creation of the WTO. In 1995, the WTO officially replaced GATT as the world's global trading body.

The goal of the WTO is in some ways consistent with the concept of Conscientious Equity: to employ a multilateral system among its member states (currently one hundred and fifty-three nations, which account for ninety-seven percent of the world's international commerce) that normalizes the rules of commerce among these nations.[3] As a member state, a WTO country must make WTO rules part of its own legal system. If a country is a member of the WTO, the laws written into its own constitution cannot supersede the laws of the WTO. The core idea—to create equitable business arrangements for all nations, along with guidelines regarding labor rights, environmental protections, and rules regarding intellectual property—is an admirable one. Unfortunately, it isn't a workable one.

The most unworkable thing about the WTO is how it makes its laws.[4] The WTO requires consensus on all decisions. That means that if even one member nation opposes a law, the law does not go into effect. The same is true with the settlement of trade disputes. If one member nation claims that another member nation is putting up barriers to trade, every member nation must agree that this is the case before the WTO imposes trade sanctions on the offending country. As you can imagine, this system allows grudges and differences in ideology to play a prominent role in all decision making.

As we saw in Seattle (and have seen in other cities around the world during WTO conferences), everyone has something to complain about with regard to the WTO. Human and labor rights activists feel that the organization foments abuses through rulings such as the one that states that governments cannot consider "noncommercial values" (such as child labor abuses) when making purchasing decisions. Environmentalists believe that the WTO makes it impossible to enact meaningful local and national environmental laws, because it advocates the removal of all barriers to trade and would consider stricter environmental laws such a barrier. Owners of small and medium-sized businesses feel that the WTO unfairly favors large corporations. Finally, developing countries believe that the WTO works solely in the interests of rich countries and establishes regulations that make it nearly impossible for developing countries to further their development.

Meanwhile, the WTO doesn't come close to fulfilling its original charter. Although the operating principle of the organization is to level the playing field among all participants in international trade, it has not succeeded. The simple fact is that the "most favored nations" status that the WTO insists all member nations extend to other member nations does nothing to prevent a country from putting up enormous barriers to entry—as long as they put up those barriers to everyone. Therefore, nations such as Brazil and India can get away with intensely protectionist policies and still have access to the lower duties and tariffs imposed by other countries (such as the United States). The WTO has done nothing to address this inequity. All it has done is insist that a nation deal with all other nations equally—with one huge exception, which I will discuss shortly.

The WTO is essentially a haywire version of the United Nations. Like the United Nations, it does a great deal of grandstanding and pulpit pounding. Like the United Nations, it is largely incapable of exerting its will on nations that choose to ignore its dictates. Yet the WTO is even more pernicious, more capable of gumming up the works with its bureaucracy, and more disposed to allow feuds and agendas to affect its policies.

## HOW DID WE GET INTO THIS MESS?

The United States was one of the original nations to agree to GATT and is a charter member of the WTO. As such, Americans have turned our trade sovereignty over to a multinational organization that couldn't possibly have our best interests at heart and that has given clear indications of anti-Americanism. Although some might suggest that countries with large, rich economies such as the United States impose undue influence on the WTO, this is decidedly not the case.

Consider, for instance, the judgment of the WTO against the United States in a dispute with Antigua and Barbuda, a nation of seventy thousand people. Antigua and Barbuda claimed that U.S. laws against offshore Internet gambling put up unfair barriers to entry.[5] The United States argued that WTO laws did not cover gambling and that the United States had established its Internet gambling laws to prevent children from gaining easy access to these sites. The WTO accepted neither argument and demanded that the United States allow offshore Internet gambling sites full access to American computers. When the United States failed to comply, the WTO took an extraordinary step—it allowed Antigua and Barbuda, in essence, to steal up to twenty-one million dollars in American intellectual property per year without punishment.[6]

In the face of a case as outrageous as this one, I can only ask, "What have we been thinking?" with regard to our relationship with the WTO. As I discussed in the last chapter and as will certainly become clearer to you as you read further into this book, our international commerce policies have at least as much to do with our national security as do our armed forces and our intelligence agencies. Enormous trade deficits put us in a tenuous position with countries like China and Japan. This threat looms as large as any military threat we face and may even present a weak spot where damage could be inflicted on us suddenly and devastatingly. Yet we have given the WTO complete responsibility for protecting us on the world trade front. This is tantamount to turning our military defense over to the United Nations.

Does anyone in America think that would be a good idea?

The WTO even reaches its tendrils into our domestic policy. Remember, WTO member nations agree that WTO law supersedes their own laws. That means that, when setting policies for our own businesses and our own communities, we need to acknowledge WTO rulings first. A particularly outrageous example of the consequences of participation in the WTO came when the State of California rejected a "Buy California" bill (a piece of legislation that would have given a slight advantage to local businesses that pay local taxes) because it didn't conform to WTO rulings. Essentially, the California government couldn't help entrepreneurs within its own state, from which it gets its tax revenue with regard to business *being done in that state*, because of legislation created by a ruling body in Geneva.

It is easy to understand why America signed onto GATT: it tied into our post–World War II aims to reenergize the world economy. However, as I have noted of our other trade policies, by the time the WTO came along, our needs and the world's needs were very different. It is, therefore, mystifying why we would have given so much power to an organization with so little to offer us.

## THE HALCYON DAYS OF SECTION 301

The United States once had a form of protection against barriers to trade far greater than anything the WTO has ever offered. Section 301 of the Trade Act of 1974, was "the principal statutory authority under which the United States may impose trade sanctions against foreign countries that maintain barriers, policies, and practices that violate, or deny US benefits under trade agreements or restrict, burden, or discriminate against US commerce."[7] Section 301 continues:

Where USTR (the United States Trade Representative) makes an affirmative determination that an act, policy or practice is actionable under Section 301, it may suspend or withdraw trade concessions, impose duties or other import restrictions, withdraw, limit or suspend benefits under the General System of Preferences, the Caribbean Basin Economic Recovery Act, or the Andean Trade Preference Act, and negotiate agreements to eliminate or phase out the act, policy or practice or provide compensation for trade distortion.

Super 301 (an addendum to Section 301) required the USTR to publicly identify "priority foreign countries" and unfair "priority practices" that posed major obstacles to U.S. exports. If the offending country was not forthcoming in scrapping its designated barriers, Super 301 provided the president the authority to retaliate.

Super 301 led to the success of several quantifiable market-opening initiatives with Japan. President Reagan deftly used the threat of Section 301 to revalue the Japanese yen. Immediately after the Plaza Agreement in September of 1985, the yen appreciated against the U.S. dollar by more than fifty percent. This appreciation played a crucial role in increasing American exports.

Contrast this example with Beijing's refusal today to allow the grossly undervalued renminbi (RMB) to reflect its true value, thus making Chinese products artificially competitive. In another era, the American president could have invoked Section 301 to force China's hand. However, the threat of Section 301 has all but disappeared. Because of the mandates of the WTO, the United States can no longer directly apply Section 301 to pressure trading partners into eliminating barriers to U.S. exports and other unfair practices. U.S. trade enforcement is now in the hands of the WTO's Dispute Settlement Body (DSB), which essentially removes the U.S. government from the governing of its own interests in international commerce.

Our membership in the WTO has weakened and compromised us. Hoping for anything else from the organization is futile. The very charter of the WTO—which allows countries that are openly hostile to the United States to have an up-or-down vote on our policies and disputes—works against us and could never realistically change to our satisfaction. The only way to win is, as they say in the movie *War Games*, not to play the game. For the health of its economy and for the health of many of the citizens of the nations with which it does business, the United States needs to take back its trade sovereignty. As long as we rely on the WTO, our security in international commerce will always be at risk. However, there is one huge loophole in WTO law that allows us to solve this problem in the same way we can solve so many others—through Conscientious Equity Accords.

The WTO requires that each member nation offer "most favored nations" status to all other member nations, but nothing in the WTO charter prevents nations from making bilateral agreements with each other. China and the EU have used this greatly to their advantage, signing free trade agreements that lower the tariffs and duties they pay around the world without concern for the WTO's mandates or the enforcement techniques of its DSB. Therefore, our path to trade sovereignty involves sitting down at the negotiating table and hammering out Conscientious Equity Accords with each nation with which we do business, creating agreements far more comprehensive and equitable than anything the WTO could devise. This might seem cumbersome, but it is actually much more manageable than continuing along our current path. Simply put, it is more practical for us to negotiate agreements with one trade partner at a time than it is for us to attempt to do the same with one hundred and fifty-two at once via the WTO.

We need to look no further than the current round of WTO trade negotiation to see why this is the case. The Doha Development Round (so named because it began in Doha, Qatar) started in November 2001. As I write this, nearly nine years later, the WTO has been unable to accomplish anything substantial with these talks, which were aimed at lowering trade barriers throughout the world and increasing global trade. Sheila Page of the Overseas Development Institute equated the progress of the Doha Round with "watching paint that never dries."[8] Since the original Doha meetings, the round has been the focus of conversation at the WTO Ministerial Conferences in Cancun and Hong Kong, as well as at special meetings in Paris, Potsdam, and three times in Geneva.[9]

The primary source of the breakdown is the subject of agricultural subsidies. Here, the divide exists between rich entities such as the United States, Japan, and the EU, where subsidies are high (nowhere more so than in Japan), and developing nations, where subsidies depress prices at home and make it impossible to penetrate lucrative export markets.

We'll discuss agricultural subsidies at length later in this book, but the underlying point is that subsidies allow subsidized farmers to sell their goods below the cost of production. This has an impact on the price of the goods in their home market (making it more difficult for exporters to enter that market) and gives the goods a price advantage in the international market (adding to their appeal as exports). The developing countries, most of which do not subsidize their farmers, want the United States and other nations, to cut agricultural subsidies dramatically. However, they offer very little in exchange.

Exacerbating this is the fact that the leading voices for the developing countries come from Brazil and India. Brazil and India have the tenth and twelfth largest GDPs in the world respectively. Their markets are huge. They are also among those most closed to exports, with outsized tariffs, duties, and other barriers to trade. In fact, the barriers these nations erect make the Tariff of Abominations seem like duty-free commerce. Yet, when speaking for the least developed countries of the world, they have offered few concessions on their protectionist trade policies, insisting on keeping a large number of their products exempt from tariff cuts.

In addition, Brazil and India have been reluctant to offer any help in preventing intellectual property theft within their borders. The result is a standoff in which both sides have refused to blink for nearly nine years.

It would be easy to imagine this standoff extending into the next century or ending with smokescreen concessions that do little to improve trade conditions around the world. Such is the fate of progress when one tries to move one hundred and fifty-two parties in the same direction at the same time. It seems far more likely that America could negotiate one hundred and fifty-two individual Conscientious Equity Accords (far more than would actually be necessary, because several regions would band together under one agreement, such as the free trade agreement we have with the nations of Central America) than that the WTO could ever create an environment that allowed fair and equitable commerce throughout the world.

Like the United Nations, the WTO isn't going anywhere. Its presence on the world stage is too large, and the politics involved in extricating oneself from it are too punitive for it to disappear. Also like the UN, the WTO functions best as a ceremonial entity. Just as we would never allow the UN to protect us militarily, we cannot continue to allow the WTO to pretend to protect us commercially.

In the world of international commerce, the WTO is not the answer. Nor is rioting on the streets of Seattle (or wherever the WTO convention travels) to demand that it address all of our social ills.

Conscientious Equity can be the solution to a complicated problem.

## CHAPTER FOUR

# PLAYING BY THE RULES WHEN THE RULES DON'T EXIST

I VISITED JAKARTA, INDONESIA, FOR THE FIRST TIME nearly thirty years ago, when I was an idealistic and impressionable young man at the start of my career in international business. Upon arriving, I checked into one of the city's most luxurious hotels and headed straight to the concierge to inquire where I could see a live performance of gamelan. Gamelan is a form of Indonesian music (with Balinese and Javanese analogs) dating back to the twelfth century. Kneeling musicians in colorful batiks play xylophones, drums, gongs, and other percussion instruments tuned to unique scales, making their melodies unpredictable and strangely pleasing. The driving rhythms and intense clashing sounds are punctuated by long climaxing crescendos. Gamelan musicians often provide the soundtrack to the ancient Indonesian puppet theater art form known as *wayang*. The gamelan ensemble performs as the puppet masters and their carved, colorful puppets act out Hindu-Buddhist stories about nobility, complete with princesses in distress and their royal saviors. I'd been exposed to this exotic (to my ears) form of music in college, and the sound of gamelan always conjured up paradisiacal images of musicians in bright Asian attire playing as the sun set on another beautiful island evening. I couldn't wait to experience this in person.

Based on his confused reaction, it was clear that the concierge wasn't accustomed to hearing such a request from a hotel patron. However, he seemed pleased to address it, lighting up with a contagious smile and taking out a Bahasa Indonesia–language newspaper. The paper indicated that there was a performance that evening not far away.

After he pulled out this information, the concierge quickly grew serious. He warned me that the concert was in a part of town that foreigners rarely visited and that I should not be strolling around there by myself. He strongly suggested that I take a hotel car and have the driver wait for me until the show ended.

A few hours later, the driver took me to a decaying theater. In my mind, I'd envisioned a Broadway spectacle, but I began to understand that my imaginings had been terribly naive. Small folding chairs were jammed together in neat rows. The only relief from the stifling heat and humidity were the large rickety ceiling fans that churned above. I felt the weight of hundreds of pairs of eyes peering at me through the haze of Kretek cigarettes and the toxic fumes emanating from open sewers all around us.

I felt vulnerable in a way I could never remember feeling, and I furtively glanced about to see if I could locate the driver who had agreed to wait for me outside the theater. What if something happened to me? What if the driver had taken my money and left me there to fend for myself? I had no clue how to get back to the hotel, and I couldn't speak a word of Bahasa Indonesia. But I was there to enjoy an unusual musical experience, to which I had been looking forward from the moment I had learned that I was going to Jakarta. I had taken a giant risk, but I couldn't let fear and distrust get in the way of the experience.

As I sat waiting for the performance to begin, two things struck me. One was that I was the only Caucasian in the audience. Considering what the concierge had told me, this did not surprise me. The other was that a level of poverty surrounded me that I'd never witnessed before. The people's clothes, their environs, and the blank looks of submission on their faces told me that the attendees of this concert had very, very little—and no hope of ever improving their lot. Even more striking, I was sitting amongst people who at least had enough money to pay to see this concert. That meant that these weren't the poorest of the poor in Jakarta.

This experience left a permanent mark on my conscience. It wasn't exactly compassion for these poor and destitute souls that I felt at that moment; compassion would come later. Rather, I was angry and disgusted that people could live in such dire poverty, and even more by the notion that these people seemed completely resigned to their miserable existences. The gamelan performance was a rare respite for them. When the show ended, they would go back to lives, too resigned to muster even a sense of desperation. I still found the music astounding that night, but I never forgot for a second how starkly the vision of this moment I had imagined contrasted with the everyday reality of the audience. I couldn't dream of living day after day in the conditions they did. I felt an urge to help them, to do something to alleviate their plight, but I didn't know what I could do.

The following morning, while standing on the balcony of my elegant seventeenth-floor room, I surveyed the sights of the kampong (shantytown) only minutes from the hotel grounds. Orange clay roofs stretched for several blocks. These roofs covered shacks with dirt floors and no running water. A putrid, brown river swerved through the kampong, bubbles frothing on the surface as the garbage in the water decayed. Skimpily dressed children waded in this water and splashed each other. At times, they would fall and disappear underneath the brown murkiness before quickly reappearing, laughing uncontrollably. Some women crouched over tin basins to wash clothes, while others built small fires from dried wood to cook their evening meals in stockpots filled with the sludge. This open cesspool was both life and death to these people.

The vision tore at me. I wanted to run down to the river's edge and shake those mothers until they realized what this diseased water was doing to them and their children. I wanted to shout at the top of my lungs that their daily routines led to high infant mortality and ceaseless instances of deadly illness. I didn't do anything of the sort, though, because I knew even then that these women had no choice.

And they never would.

As I drove around the Indonesian cities of Jakarta, Surabaya, and Medan, the vastness of the poverty I saw stunned me. What I'd witnessed at the river's edge was not unique, nor was it unique to Indonesia. I saw similar atrocities in the Philippines, Thailand, Sri Lanka, India, Pakistan, Africa, and Latin America. Everywhere I traveled, I was haunted by grinding, halting, hideous poverty.

A few years later, I moved into a highly secure compound in Manila. A number of prominent Philippine political figures, including President Estrada, were my neighbors. Our "village" was surrounded by high concrete block walls with charred glass cemented into the top. Should any poor fools try to make it over the walls, they would slash themselves and, perhaps, bleed to death. If, somehow, they managed to reach the other side alive, they would have to contend with our guards carrying Uzi machine guns and 12-gauge, double-barreled, sawed-off shotguns. This was a crazy time of almost daily kidnappings and "sparrow units" sent by the Communist New People's Army to assassinate Americans. Because I was a high-value target, our guards were to shoot first and ask questions later.

A large shantytown that sprang up just outside our walls was home to countless faceless people. They used anything and everything imaginable to construct their shacks. I lived less than a hundred feet away, but I never knew any of their names.

Poverty is much worse than having no food, medicine, or clean water. It goes well beyond having no shelter, education, or access to healthcare. Poverty is living in a continuous state of abuse from the moment you are born to the time that you die.

If these poor children are not killed by the diseased waters where they play and that they drink, they often fall victim to child abuse, both physical and sexual, that is passed from one generation to the next. Maybe because of their own hopelessness and despair, parents take out their anger on those least able to defend themselves.

Daughters become the family breadwinners at young ages. Having an attractive daughter is a godsend, as she can be sent to work in nightclubs, hostess bars, and massage parlors, selling herself so her family can eat and her siblings can go to school. You can't help but be stunned by the number of parents who feel forced to "sell" their children for just a few dollars. An attractive woman with no resources of her own may often become the mistress of a married man of means. When he no longer finds the woman attractive, she sends her young daughter to take her place in the bedroom and save their lives. Like other the cycles of abuse, this cycle perpetuates itself over generations.

I first arrived in Southeast Asia as a young American entrepreneur full of big ideas to save the world. I often believed it was my life's mission to save the poor, one by one if I had to. However, after living with poverty and witnessing its devastation every day, I found that, instead of caring, I'd begun to gaze over the heads of the desperately poor to avoid them. This must be some sort of subconscious survival mechanism. When you become consumed with the hopelessness of the situation, it weighs down on your conscience and frustrates you. You realize that poverty and corruption feed on each other in a self-perpetuating cycle. To succeed in this environment as a businessperson, you must participate in this process, even if you find that it is reprehensible and makes you feel less human.

There seems to be no room for idealism in countries overrun by corruption and greed. Consider the customs officer, internal revenue official, member of the judiciary, or government worker who earns less than a hundred dollars a month while trying to raise a family and support elderly parents. Under this person's control are documents that can have a major impact on financial issues and people's lives. Others are constantly tempting such individuals with big money, usually many times their monthly salaries, to simply look the other way. Given their situation, how could they turn down such an offer? In a nation where the rulers were corrupt, business leaders were corrupt, and your boss and co-workers were corrupt, do you think you would act differently?

Over time, I came to understand the hopeless plight of those trapped in poverty. The more successful I became as an American exporter, the more I had to deal with corruption. Just as poverty is omnipresent, so is dark, deceitful corruption lurking around every corner. To repeatedly face down corruption will change you forever. The countless millions of mothers I have seen on the river's edge have no chance for a better life. The resources needed to provide clean water, sewer systems, healthcare, education, and nutrition are being sucked out of the economy through the enormous cost of corruption.

Sadly, the wails of mothers who have lost their infant children to disease because they lack the most basic services do not reach the ears of those in Merdeka Palace in Jakarta, Malacanang Palace in Manila, or all the other presidential palaces in poverty-stricken nations. I have met many government and military leaders of developing nations who give lip service to poverty alleviation but adamantly embrace corruption, its sinister enabler. The culture of corruption runs deep. It is expected by family, friends, and colleagues that, when attaining a position of authority, one maximizes the financial gain it brings.

Is gripping poverty a result of corruption, or is rampant corruption fueled by abject poverty? This is a tough circle to square.

## POVERTY AND CORRUPTION

I could go on for hundreds of pages recounting stories of the tragic poverty that I have witnessed in my travels around the world and even in America. It seems to be an immutable law that a huge percentage of the world's population should go through life penniless. As I have already noted, nearly half of the people living on this planet right now must try to get by on less than two dollars a day. The problem seems too great for us even to consider a solution. Yet we could go a long way toward changing the fates of so many of these people—while at the same time improving conditions for the average American—if we were to take a Conscientious Equity stand against corruption, one of the most pernicious contributors to poverty.

There is a clear connection between poverty and corruption. In a recent *Forbes* article, Michael Johnston, a professor at Colgate University, noted:

The links between corruption and poverty affect both individuals and businesses, and they run in both directions: poverty invites corruption, while corruption deepens poverty. Corruption both causes and thrives upon weaknesses in key economic, political, and social institutions. It is a form of self-serving influence akin to a heavily regressive tax, benefiting the haves at the expense of the have-nots. Trust—essential to financial markets and effective governments everywhere—is difficult to build in poor and corrupt societies.[1]

In a 2003 address, then–Secretary General of the UN Kofi Annan underscored this connection:

> Corruption hurts poor people in developing countries dispropor-
> tionately. It affects their daily life in many different ways, and tends
> to make them even poorer, by denying them their rightful share of
> economic resources or life-saving aid. Corruption puts basic public
> services beyond the reach of those who cannot afford to pay bribes.
> By diverting scarce resources intended for development, corrup-
> tion also makes it harder to meet fundamental needs such as those
> for food, health, and education. It creates discrimination between
> the different groups in society, feeds inequality and injustice, dis-
> courages foreign investment and aid, and hinders growth. It is,
> therefore, a major obstacle to political stability, and to successful
> social and economic development.[2]

Corruption is an impediment to healthy business practices every-where, but it absolutely imprisons the poverty-stricken. Corrupt officials force the poor to pay bribes for healthcare, police assis-tance, and even access to education. Corrupt government leaders accept kickbacks from foreign contractors, denying their own peo-ple the opportunity to earn a living wage in construction and man-ufacturing. Corrupt agreements and price fixing prevent farmers from selling their produce at decent prices even within their own countries.

Transparency International is a global organization leading the fight against corruption. Its primary purpose is to raise awareness of corrupt practices around the world. One of the most power-ful documents that Transparency International has created is its Corruption Perceptions Index (CPI), which ranks countries based on a number of factors that contribute to corruption. Transparency International asserts that the CPI "measures the perceived levels of public-sector corruption in a given country and is a composite index, drawing on different expert and busi-ness surveys."[3] In its 2008 CPI, Denmark, New Zealand, and Sweden tied as the least corrupt nations (the United States tied for eighteenth among the one hundred and eighty countries ranked), and Somalia, Myanmar, and Iraq were the most corrupt. To drive home the connection between corruption and poverty, these three countries on the bottom of the list were, respectively, the two-hundred-and-nineteenth, one-hundred-and-seventy-ninth, and one-hundred and-fifty-first poorest countries (based on GDP) of the two hundred and twenty-five countries measured by the CIA World Factbook.[4]

## KINGS OF THE CORRUPT

Transparency International has regularly ranked the Philippines and Indonesia among the world's most corrupt nations. In the 2008 CPI, the Philippines showed up at one hundred forty-one (or thirty-ninth most corrupt among the one hundred eighty studied), and Indonesia hit the list at one hundred twenty-six (or fifty-fourth most corrupt), so they still have some work to do if they want to make it to the top. However, these countries hold the dubi-ous distinction of being homes to the leaders that Transparency International rank as the two most corrupt in the history of the world.

President Haji Mohamed Suharto ruled Indonesia from 1967–1998. Transparency International estimates that Suharto embez-zled more money than any world leader ever did—more than seventy-three billion dollars slipped into his hands and those of his family members. His wife, Madame Tien Suharto, was so monumentally corrupt that she earned the nickname "Madame Ten Percent," in reference to how she skimmed money off the top of so many Indonesian transactions.

As I quickly learned from working in Indonesia during the Suharto regime, in order to maintain a successful business presence there, I needed to set aside my moral objections and play the game. At the time, I was bidding on large commercial foodservice equipment contracts. Those with whom I worked in the country told me several times that I needed to increase the pricing on these bids to accommodate members of the Suharto family. This sickened me because I knew that I was playing into the cycle of corruption that generated the poverty I had witnessed as an impressionable young man on my first trip to Indonesia. Yet I had to make payroll. Such is the slippery slope on which exporters regularly find themselves.

Singapore's former prime minister and elder statesman Lee Kuan Yew revealed in his memoirs that, during the Asian economic crisis in 1998, he told members of the Suharto family that international fund managers were paying careful attention to the economic privileges the Suharto children enjoyed. He told them that their control of almost everything created a total loss of confidence in the economic soundness of Indonesia. With equal frankness, the Suharto daughters responded that they could not and would not accept his advice to step down their corrupt practices. Because of their greed, the rupiah (the Indonesian currency) went into a freefall, and business came to a grinding halt. This led to tens of millions of poor Indonesians sinking even deeper into poverty.

In 2002, an Indonesian court sentenced the favorite son of former President Suharto to fifteen years in jail for paying a hit man to kill a Supreme Court judge.[5] The judge had sentenced Tommy Suharto to eighteen months in prison over a multimillion-dollar real estate scam. When Tommy could not overturn the conviction by bribing the judge, he ordered the judge's assassination instead. Since a murder charge carries the maximum penalty of death, the fifteen-year sentence (which the courts subsequently reduced to ten years) was an obvious nod to the power the Suhartos once wielded. Tommy Suharto is the first and only member of the Suharto family to be jailed for a criminal offense. He went free on October 30, 2006, after serving only four years of his sentence. There is no clear evidence that this happened because of money paid to a member of the administration of current President Susilo "Bambang" Yudhoyono. However, there is plenty of speculation.

The Political and Economic Risk Consultancy recently listed the Indonesian Supreme Court as the most corrupt in Asia. I have seen first-hand that this corruption pervades the entire Indonesian legal system. During the Suharto years, my company received a substantial contract for a resort hotel under construction in Manado, an island at the eastern end of the archipelago. Unfortunately, we had to bring legal proceedings against the owner to collect our final payment. We retained the Jakarta branch of one of the largest and most respected American law firms. After a year of preparation for litigation, the firm dropped our case without explanation. I have reason to believe that our lawyers were physically threatened and decided that it was unsafe to proceed.

Shortly afterward, a court in Jakarta sent down a judgment *against* our company for several hundred thousand dollars. There was no trial, there were no briefs, and we made no appearances. All we received was a ruling stating that I needed to fork over the cash or face serious consequences. Luck was with me in this case, though. Soon after the ruling, the government of President Suharto collapsed, and the judges went running for cover. I have not heard anything further about this, but I know several people who face similarly outrageous rulings under the current government.

Ferdinand Marcos of the Philippines fell short in his quest to be the ultimate king of the corrupt, as Transparency International ranks him second to Suharto. The estimated twenty billion he stole puts him light years behind Suharto's record-setting pace. In the annals of corruption, he'll always be no better than a silver medalist.

Ferdinand Marcos had modest personal financial resources before winning the presidency in 1965. This was quickly to change, as he and his wife ran the Philippines as their own personal piggy bank. In 1998, Imelda Marcos declared in an interview with a local newspaper, "We practically own everything in the Philippines from electricity, telecommunications, airlines, banking, beer and tobacco, newspaper publishing, television stations, shipping, oil, mining, hotels and resorts, coconut and sugar mills, small firearms, real estate and insurance."[6]

As in Indonesia, I had to set aside my moral objections when seeking to secure business in the Philippines. Because of currency restrictions and because the Philippine peso is not easily convertible into hard currency, it was very difficult for the ruling elite and business community to get U.S. dollars out of the Philippines. A practice used extensively to remedy this problem was "salting" contracts. During the time of the Marcos regime, contracts were routinely overstated and signed off by the central bank before making transfers to banks outside the country, to accounts inevitably controlled by the Marcos family and their cronies. If a fair contract value was $1,000,000, a contract for $1,800,000 would be submitted. The excess served as "commissions" to individuals with close ties to Marcos. This practice, although illegal, was so widespread that everyone knew what was going on. Even the American government—still the shadow government presence there at the time—turned a blind eye.

In 1986, during the final days of the Marcos government, the People Power Revolution against the corruption that Marcos represented boiled over. Angry mobs approached the Malacanang Presidential Palace, where Marcos and his family hunkered down. Marcos called his friend and confidant U.S. Senator Paul Laxalt. Laxalt told Marcos that the time had come to "cut and cut cleanly."[7] Laxalt was saying that Marcos no longer had the support of the United States. Sixteen hours later, U.S. military helicopters evacuated Marcos from Malacanang, and Marcos began his exile in Hawaii. Immediately after the helicopters lifted off, angry mobs of the People Power Revolution and tore down the gates of Malacanang and ransacked the palace.

At its core, the People Power Revolution was an explosive release of festering outrage. On the surface, it was an iconic battle of good against evil. Massive crowds shouted "Cory,...Cory,...Cory" hysterically, as though they could turn their chants into bullets fired at the hearts of Marcos and his cronies. Their pent-up anger had exploded when Marcos henchmen had assassinated Cory Aquino's husband, opposition leader Senator Benigno "Ninoy" Aquino, upon his arrival home after a three-year exile in the United States. I remember standing on a balcony overlooking Roxas Boulevard as the funeral procession passed below. I have never again witnessed such a spontaneous emotional outpouring by a sea of people.

President Corazon Aquino was ushered into power in 1986 on a platform of ending corruption and bringing about lasting land reform. Executive Order #1 established the Presidential Commission on Good Governance (PCGG) to restore to the Philippines the vast amounts of wealth stolen by Marcos and his cohorts. Sadly, the commission recovered very little, and no one in the Marcos inner circle spent a night in jail for their blatant crimes and plunder.

What is more amazing is how soon people forget. A common trait found in seriously corrupt countries is how difficult it is to break the pattern. It is akin to the cycle of abused children becoming abusive parents. Although Cory Aquino has the image of a simple, devout Catholic housewife who suddenly rose to save her country from tyranny and chaos, she was herself from the powerful Cojuangco Clan of Tarlac province, one of the richest families in the Philippines. Hacienda Luisita, which Aquino's family owns, is a lasting symbol of feudalism and oligarchy. It spans more than thirteen thousand acres and more than five thousand farmers and their families (more than thirty thousand people total) live there in modern-day serfdom.

A court ruled in 1985 that haciendas throughout the Philippines must be parceled out to the poor farmers who have worked the land for generations. Then, Aquino became president. She inserted a provision into the 1987 constitution that exempted land-owning corporations from agrarian reform, provided they give out shares instead. Taking advantage of this loophole, Hacienda Luisita granted company stock to its farmers on an installment basis. However, the voting rights remained with the Cojuangcos until the farmers could pay for the stock. Since the farmers earned sub-humane incomes, they would never be able to make these payments.

At the end of 2004, the five thousand farmers living on starvation wages were in a deadlock with Hacienda Luisita management on a number of issues. These issues included the dismissal of several farmers, who were replaced by those from more impoverished provinces who were willing to work for less. The farmers felt there was no way to push their cause other than to strike. The violent dispersal of the strike on November 16, 2004, by the Cojuangcos' private army—now known as the Luisita Massacre—led to the death of fourteen residents, including women and children, and the wounding of more than two hundred others.

Today, many of the best-known Marcos cronies, who stole billions of dollars from the Philippine people, are back in positions of power. Edward Cojuangco (a cousin of Cory Aquino), who controlled the coconut monopoly for Marcos, today controls San

Miguel Corporation, the largest and most prestigious Philippine corporation. Lucio Tan owns Fortune Tobacco and Asian Brewery and controls Philippine Airlines. Two of the Marcos children were elected to public office. The eldest daughter, Aimee, served three terms as a congresswoman for Ilocos Norte province, and the Marcoses' son Bongbong is currently a congressman and former governor of Ilocos Norte.

The Marcoses are not the only corrupt political family to return to power. Joseph Estrada was elected president of the Philippines in 1998. On the few occasions I have met President Estrada, he has mumbled his words and had a hard time speaking in complete sentences. He had a perpetual glassy look in his eyes, as if he'd been on a nonstop bender. I have seen him so inebriated that I was convinced that the slightest gust of wind would knock him over. Estrada was overthrown by street protests in 2001 and arrested for plunder and running a gambling ring. This would seem to suggest progress. However, the country elected both the wife and son of disgraced President Estrada to the Senate.

In the elections of May 2010, Benigno Aquino III was elected as the fifteenth president of the Philippines. Coming in second was Joseph Estrada, recently released from house arrest.

## CORRUPTION IN OTHER PARTS OF THE WORLD

For many, Nigeria, one of Africa's richest and most powerful countries, is the definition of corruption.

Since 1960, when Nigeria gained independence from Britain, it is estimated that Nigeria's rulers have stolen more than four hundred billion dollars. To put this in context, this is roughly the equivalent of all the aid the West has sent to the entire continent of Africa in that time. When the G-8 leaders discussed a Marshall Plan for Africa at their 2005 summit in Scotland,

Nigeria's rulers had already taken for themselves six times as much money as the G-8 countries were planning to provide to the entire region.

Nigeria's corruption is far reaching and occurs openly. Upon arrival at Lagos International Airport as a young recent college grad, I had a small problem with my vaccination papers. Officials held me in a room until they could page the Nigerian chief I was visiting in the arrivals area. Things moved quickly after that. The chief simply handed the immigration officer a wad of naira, and I was happily on my way.

Many of Nigeria's leaders are schooled in the United States and England. They would never think of behaving as they do in Nigeria while living overseas. Once they arrive back home, however, their demeanor and actions change radically. They have complete disregard for their fellow citizens when it comes to enriching themselves.

Some Nigerians have tried to tell me that the country's endemic corruption and poverty result from colonialism. They argue that Nigeria was created by the British to secure their economic dominance and that the three major tribes of Nigeria are incompatible and would not be one nation if not for the manipulation of the British. I don't buy it. Many countries with colonial pasts control corruption effectively. Singapore, Hong Kong, the United Arab Emirates, Botswana, and Malaysia are all clean countries according to Transparency International. Furthermore, the Nigerians fail to recognize that *Nigerian chiefs* were selling their own people into slavery well before they were colonized. The fact is that the leaders of African nations are anti-African. They despise and discriminate against their own people. They have no second thoughts about doing so.

In Latin America, Transparency International lists Venezuela as one of the most seriously corrupt nations. Like Indonesia and Nigeria, Venezuela is a rich country and a member of OPEC. Since Hugo Chavez took power in 1998, corruption has become much more widespread and openly practiced. Because the government controls everything, there is no limit to the amount of corruption possible. Only the Catholic Church has had the guts to say anything about it.

One trick that Chavez and his military thugs employ comes straight out of the Corrupt Despotic Rulers Handbook. The Internal Revenue Department imposes an outrageous tax assessment on a targeted company. This leads to trumped-up charges of tax evasion that make the evening news. The company's owners feel vulnerable and agree to sell their business for well below its market value. Chavez then uses the profits to fund his radical form of nouveaux-Castro ideology.

Although U.S. officials are nowhere near the stratosphere of these corruption kings, I must point out that we're far from immune to corruption. There are disturbing developments within our country that we must watch carefully. According to the U.S. Census Bureau, in 2006 (the most recent year for which statistics are available), 36.5 million Americans, or 12.3 percent of the population, were living below the poverty line. As I have established, poverty and corruption go hand in hand.

One of the most recent and harrowing examples of the presence of poverty in the United States was the devastation wreaked by Hurricane Katrina. According to the *New York Times*, the *Detroit Free Press*, and the Brookings Institution, Katrina killed more than sixteen hundred people, displaced about a million, and destroyed some two hundred thousand Gulf Coast homes. News reports place insured property damage at 25.3 billion dollars. There were 1.7 million insurance claims, nine hundred and seventy-five thousand of them from Louisiana. As I write this, more than four years later, rebuilding remains spotty, despite one hundred ten billion dollars in federal monies allocated to the task.

There is an ongoing downward shift in American incomes. As such, there will also be a substantial increase in the number of Americans in the lower middle class who are just barely making it.

Corruption in the United States is likely to accelerate at all levels. The implications are truly scary.

## WHY THE FCPA ISN'T WORKING

In the mid-1970s, the Securities and Exchange Commission (SEC) launched an investigation into the practices of American businesses on foreign soil. What it uncovered—no surprise to any of you who have read this far—was more than four hundred U.S. companies that "admitted making questionable or illegal payments in excess of $300 million to foreign government officials, politicians, and political parties."[8] The result of this investigation was the Foreign Corrupt Practices Act of 1977 (FCPA). The act sought to prevent American firms from paying bribes to foreign officials and carried with it strong penalties for violators, including fines, jail sentences, and disbarment from federal procurement contracting.

The FCPA was enough of a threat that it curtailed "business as usual" for many American companies dealing with corrupt governments. The problem was that it increased the unevenness of the playing field for American exporters. Other countries turned a blind eye to bribery if bribes generated business. Some even allowed companies to deduct the payment of bribes on their taxes. In an intensely competitive universe, the FCPA made American companies less competitive.

Understandably, the American government did not think repealing the FCPA was the best response to this problem. This would have been tantamount to announcing, "Never mind; go ahead and bribe whomever you need to bribe." Instead, the government sought a way to convince other countries to adopt the same standards that we had with the FCPA. This led to the Organization of Economic Cooperation and Development Convention on Combating Bribery of Foreign Public Officials in International

Business Transactions. The countries that have ratified the convention (thirty-seven to date, including most of the EU, Japan, South Korea, Canada, Mexico, several South American countries with large economies, and others—but notably not China, and certainly not any of the countries we discussed earlier in this chapter) have agreed to create anti-bribing legislation.[9] Unfortunately, various countries' definitions of "anti-bribing legislation" leave much room for interpretation.

## CONSCIENTIOUS EQUITY AS A CURB TO CORRUPTION

My exposure to poverty and corruption have had a profound impact on me and inspired the development of Conscientious Equity. As a young American idealist, I could do nothing to improve the situation of those who needed our help the most. I could only observe and participate in the system that perpetuates the status quo. The only way that we as Americans can help bring about meaningful alleviation of poverty is by embracing the tenets of Conscientious Equity and making deals with our trading partners that have at their core enforceable measures that directly address corruption.

Our trade agreements already have clauses dealing with legal issues such as due process, environmental protections, and labor rights. We must now go further. It is only logical that we go one step further and make corruption eradication integral to our trade agreements. Foreign government, military, and business leaders will not do this by themselves. They are as numb to poverty and corruption as I became. They have huge a financial interest in keeping things just as they are. However, there are many good-intentioned civil servants who would mandate real change if their trade relationships with the United States were at risk.

This means we must vigorously pursue Conscientious Equity Accords with all of our trading partners, especially those with ingrained corrupt practices. We must forestall the growth of corruption in our own country by insisting on the same access to foreign markets for manufactured goods as we allow here. Doing so will bring economic activity back to our poorest regions, including Appalachia, those affected by Hurricane Katrina, the embattled industrial Midwest, and others.

You have read this already in this book and you are going to read it again in future chapters because the point is too critical to minimize: we have extraordinary leverage with our trading partners because the American market is the richest and most appealing market in the world. Therefore, we are in the unique position of being able to dictate the conditions on which our trading partners trade with us—as long as we are bold enough to do so. By extension, this means that we offer the best opportunity for curbing corruption and making huge strides in alleviating poverty worldwide.

As noted earlier, our existing free trade agreements cover territory that ranges far beyond tariffs and duties. They address labor rights, environmental standards, and intellectual property protection, among other things. It is interesting to note that of the seventeen countries with which we currently have FTAs, only four fall into the bottom half of Transparency International's CPI. These are Guatemala (ninety-six), the Dominican Republic (one hundred and two), Honduras (one hundred and twenty-six), and Nicaragua (one hundred and thirty-four). All of them were part of our CAFTA agreement that also included the low-corruption countries Costa Rica and El Salvador. CAFTA includes languages regarding transparency and due process. These are decent first steps in the effort to alleviate corruption. However, our Conscientious Equity Accords need to be much more comprehensive. We need to define the rule of law much more clearly, and we need to be willing to stand behind the protections we include in these agreements.

Corruption reduction needs to be a critical component of the Conscientious Equity Accords we draft with all of our trading partners. These accords must include strict language that forces the nations that engage in commerce with us not only to deal with American companies without demanding bribes, kickbacks, and other considerations, but also to police themselves better and, most important, to give their own citizens a fair opportunity to earn a respectable wage and to sell what they produce in their homeland and, where possible, around the world.

Some might criticize this strategy as America attempting to throw its weight around and interfering in the policies of sovereign nations, but I find such criticism preposterous. What we're talking about here goes right to the heart of Conscientious Equity—giving every citizen of the world, regardless of borders, the opportunity to live a decent life. As Americans, we believe that this is every person's inalienable right. It is well within our rights—it is, in fact, our responsibility—to say to all of our trading partners, "If you want access to our extraordinarily lucrative market, then you're going to have to treat your citizens the way all human beings should be treated." It is conceivable that a country would have such a deep-seated commitment to corrupt behavior that it would risk doing business with America to maintain it, but my guess is that most of our trading partners would acquiesce.

Therefore, we must make this part of the boilerplate of every Conscientious Equity Accord we sign. We need to do this so the children of Jakarta don't risk their very lives by simply playing outside. We need to do this so honest hardworking people all over the globe can hope to earn a decent living from their efforts and imagine a brighter future for their children. Finally, we need to do it so that American businesspeople never again have to compromise their convictions for the sake of a deal.

Conscientious Equity is about doing the right thing and giving everyone a stake in the world we are creating. We must make it our mission to guarantee that corruption has no role.

CHAPTER FIVE

# INGENUITY IS NOT A PUBLIC SERVICE

MY BUSINESS IS IN THE FOODSERVICE INDUSTRY. It has sent me all over the world selling equipment to high-end purchasers. One such purchaser was a Chinese official who met with me to plan a huge operation in a five-star hotel. In the course of our discussions, he said that he wanted my company to design and engineer their industrial kitchens, along with everything else related to the preparation of food at this extravagant facility.

I told him that this fell outside of the charter of my company. We didn't do this kind of thing ourselves, but we worked closely with people who did. I told him that I could take responsibility for managing the project; that I would arrange for all of the necessary mechanical, electrical, and other engineering drawings; and that these documents would guarantee that he would buy the right equipment and install it correctly and efficiently. The building of this hotel constituted a major investment, and it made sense to outfit it properly with the right products with the right capacities. Engaging an engineering firm that had no stake in what the official was purchasing would allow him to buy exactly what he needed and only that.

We were talking about a purchase of roughly two million dollars worth of equipment. On top of this, the engineering work—a major undertaking—would cost approximately sixty thousand dollars. At about three percent of the purchase price, this was a very reasonable expense, or so it seemed to me. When I quoted the cost to the official, though, he looked at me, befuddled, and said, "We don't pay for anything that's on paper."

The idea that someone would spend money for the intellectual work of another was simply inconceivable to him.

## CREATIVE LICENSES

One could argue about whether or not America has a future as a country that makes things. Some have suggested that all of our manufacturing jobs are headed offshore and that we not only cannot stem this tide, but we should not even try. As someone who spends every day selling American-made products to other countries, I'm convinced that the United States has a rich and globally competitive future as a manufacturer and that reports of the demise of the American manufacturer are greatly exaggerated. It is important to note that America is still—by a long shot—the largest manufacturing country in the world. That's an argument for another day, though.

What is inarguable, however, is America's place in the world as a country that *creates* things. In recent years, the share of the GDP from core U.S. copyright industries grew more than twice as fast as the rest of the U.S. economy.[1] (Stephen E. Siwek of Economists Incorporated defines core copyright industries as those "whose primary purpose is to create, produce, distribute, or exhibit copyright materials. These industries include newspapers, books and periodicals, motion pictures, recorded music, music publishing, radio and television broadcasting, and business and entertainment software."[2]) In 2005, this sector represented 6.56 percent of our GDP. Taking into account the portion of other industries whose products and services derive from copyrighted material (anything from toy makers to transportation services to hardware manufacturers) makes this percentage skyrocket to 11.2 percent, or nearly a trillion and a half dollars.

American ingenuity and imagination have a huge place on the world stage. Small and medium-sized businesses generate the overwhelming percentage of this creativity, filing thirteen times more patents per employee than large corporations do. Meanwhile, the core copyright industries alone (not including the broader sector) lead all major industry sectors in U.S. exports. Our intellectual property (IP) is in demand everywhere on the globe.

Unfortunately, not everyone who demands our IP cares to pay for it. The correction of the theft of this property—especially if we were able to correct it with one particular country—would have an overwhelmingly positive impact on the American economy.

## MADE IN CHINA—WITHOUT PERMISSION

Any conversation about IP theft needs to begin with China. China is, by far, the leading source of counterfeit goods seized on attempted entry into the United States. Recent figures from the U.S. Customs and Border Protection agency indicate that China is responsible for eighty-one percent of all such goods.

Estimates put the worldwide annual value of Chinese counterfeit goods at somewhere north of three hundred and fifty billion dollars—and that's just the stolen intellectual property sold outside China's borders.[3]

Inside China, the amount of IP theft is staggering. Estimates place this cost at more than a quarter of a trillion dollars yearly for the United States. Dan Glickman, chairman and chief executive officer of the Motion Picture Association of America, believes that nine out of every ten DVDs sold in China are pirated and that the movie industry alone loses more than a quarter of a billion dollars a year to IP theft solely in China. In his 2007 statement to the congressional Committee on Ways and Means Subcommittee on Trade, Glickman called China "too frustrating to deal with, too lucrative to ignore." He added:

> While you can see virtually any US film you want in China, in pirated form, the legitimate market is one of the world's most restricted. The pirates have a thriving market, but our companies—who invest millions and employ hundreds of thousands of American workers—are throttled. The Chinese government decides which US films Chinese audiences will see, when they will see them, and dictates the terms of getting those films into China .... At the same time, as one of the fastest growing markets in the world populated with audiences who genuinely like and flock to US films, China is indeed "too [potentially] lucrative to ignore."[4]

Glickman became so concerned with rampant piracy in China that he decided to make multiple visits to the country to examine the level of counterfeiting personally. In his statement to the committee, he speaks about his first such visit:

> I visited a shop near the hotel. To my astonishment, I found a copy of one my son's movies. I met with the mayor of Beijing later that

day. The next day, the shop was raided and closed. During my next trip to China, I visited the same shop. It was full of more pirated discs. We alerted the authorities; it was raided, again, and closed. Last December, our staff met with Ministry of Culture officials, who touted the closure of the shop and its conversion to a clothing store. They visited the store, and from the outside, it did appear to be a clothing store. However, inside, in a backroom, pirate versions of virtually every current US movie remained available.

The motion picture industry is hardly alone in suffering profound losses from piracy in China. American authorities estimate that ninety percent of all business software sold in China is pirated. According to the International Federation of Phonographic Industry, piracy is responsible for ninety-five percent of music sales in China.[5] Meanwhile, a recent report in *China Daily* states that China produces five hundred million books a year without payment to the copyright holder to go along with the one hundred and twenty million counterfeit audio and video products it produces annually.[6]

Extending beyond these fields, the piracy story continues to grow. China is a leading source of counterfeit automotive parts, and the WHO lists China as a major producer of counterfeit and substandard medicines. In a piece for *Inc.* magazine, Ted C. Fishman, author of the bestseller *China, Inc.*, noted, "China's telecommunications giant, for example, Huawei Technologies, grew into a multibillion-dollar competitor by stealing the technology of advanced rivals, which stood by outraged and helpless."[7]

China has a long history of ignoring patents and trademarks, and the Chinese government has even set up a procedure to facilitate this process for IP thieves. Beginning in 2002, China required that a wide range of mechanical products—everything from televisions to microwave ovens to electrical wires to smoke detectors to X-ray equipment—carry the China Compulsory Certification

(CCC) in order to be sold within China's borders.[8] The Chinese government demands a level of documentation before it awards a CCC mark that goes far beyond what most countries request for certification. In fact, it calls for so much documentation that it essentially insists that manufacturers present all of their proprietary design work in digitized format for easy electronic transmittal anywhere in their country. The Chinese literally ask manufacturers to provide the blueprint for the piracy of their goods. The people within the Chinese government holding on to this intellectual property—often worth millions and millions of dollars—might make one hundred fifty dollars a month. Chinese manufacturers can therefore easily tempt them with small bribes and come away with hugely valuable trademarked, trade dressed, or patented information for virtually nothing. It is as though these manufacturers feel that anything available on paper or in electronic form is automatically placed in the public domain. The CCC is an ideal way for the Chinese government to regulate trade, as it puts up significant barriers to entry while simultaneously fueling the Chinese economy through the sale of knockoffs.

I've seen particularly brazen manifestations of this practice at trade shows—even those that take place on American soil. The Chinese government often has pavilions at these shows, where Chinese companies display their replicated versions of products for which American entrepreneurs own trademarks and copyrights. The original manufacturer might be no more than a hundred meters away from this pavilion, but the Chinese companies don't even try to be circumspect. They know they don't need to be, because their government fully supports them.

Since joining the WTO, the Chinese government has proclaimed a desire to do a better job of policing piracy. It has instituted new laws aimed at discouraging IP theft. However, these laws have very little practical value and absolutely no teeth. "The availability of law is not the problem—it's the remedies," says Hong Kong–based lawyer Peter Bullock. "The problem is that enforcement is patchy and the penalties awarded as damages negligible."[9] A Chinese court might find one Chinese citizen guilty of piracy, but the pay-out award is so paltry (sometimes in the low four figures) that the penalties serve as no impediment whatsoever. In fact, considering the profits that pirates glean from their crimes, they can easily factor any such judgments against them as a cost of doing business.

Calculating the amount of money lost to counterfeiting and other forms of IP theft in China is difficult. The three hundred and fifty billion dollar estimate is based on the approximate sales of the pirated goods (in other words, the price for which those goods sold). As Ted Fishman points out in his *Inc.* article, however, this is only a starting point:

> Another approach is to add up the sales that legitimate sellers would have racked up had they sold a like amount of goods at the prices they normally command. Allowing that copied goods undercut their legitimate competition by between 20 and 99 percent, the number gets huge very fast. Yet even that method doesn't begin to measure the cost to companies that dare not introduce their products to China. That price is harder to add on, since it is impossible to tally the value of plans not made. It is not hard, however, to understand that when American companies must pay full dollar for technology that Chinese companies can get for little or nothing, that dynamic can contribute to the weakening, or near disappearance, of whole American industries.

This point leads to another huge and incalculable cost of piracy. The Chinese market is massive. Even if the size of that market is grossly overstated because such a large percentage of its 1.3 billion people are not an active part of its economy, it has the third-largest GDP of any country in the world and is undeniably the fastest growing economy on the planet. Yet the threat of piracy causes an untold number of American companies to avoid competing in this market. How much is that costing us in exports and the good-paying jobs those exports generate? Our trade deficit with China in 2008 was two hundred and sixty-six billion dollars. That is an astonishing figure, one that represents a full third of our overall trade deficit. Yet the estimated two hundred and fifty billion dollars we lose every year to Chinese IP theft nearly matches it. If China dealt with us equitably, our trade deficit would all but disappear. Furthermore, if American companies felt confident about competing in China without the fear of losing their invaluable intellectual property, that deficit would very quickly turn into a surplus.

## NO ONE HOLDS THE PATENT ON IP THEFT

China steals IP at an unparalleled level. This doesn't mean that it is the only country to do so, however. Russia, for example, has little respect for copyright. A recent report in *Pravda* stated that the bulk of video and audio materials produced in Russia were counterfeit, mostly generated by the country's ubiquitous organized crime groups. Meanwhile, the Business Software Alliance claims that Russia has an eighty-seven percent piracy rate.[10]

In the spring of 2008, Susan Schwab, the U.S. Trade Representative, placed nine nations on the Priority Watch List for countries that are not doing enough to combat intellectual property crimes. China and Russia headed the list, joined by Argentina, Chile, India, Israel, Pakistan, Thailand, and Venezuela. In India, for example, a report from the International Chamber of Commerce notes, "Fast-moving consumer goods lose approximately fifteen percent of market share to counterfeits and thirty-eight percent of auto parts are fake." The same report states, "In Pakistan, piracy levels in cable television, music, and software are over ninety percent, draining more than US $1 billion in tax revenues."[11] The military regime that recently took over Thailand in a coup quickly moved to authorize pirated versions of three major pharmaceuticals produced by American and European companies.

IP theft is an issue in many corners of the globe. According to the U.S. Trade Representative's 2003 Special 301 Report, IP theft is "a massive, sophisticated global business involving the manufacturing and sale of counterfeit versions of everything from soaps, shampoos, razors, and batteries to cigarettes, alcoholic beverages, and automobile parts, as well as medicines and health care products."[12] Recently, Sebastian Wright, an international trade specialist at the U.S. Department of Commerce's Office of Intellectual Property Rights noted that seven to nine percent of all world trade involves counterfeit goods.

In 2004, Jon W. Dudas, Acting Undersecretary of Commerce for Intellectual Property and Acting Director of the United States Patent and Trademark Office, testified before the U.S. Senate Committee on Judiciary. In his statement, he said, "Today, the illegal duplication of software, music, DVDs, and other digitized information and the trafficking in counterfeit products, from which no industry and no country is exempt, are all too common."[13] Later in his statement, he added, "by all accounts counterfeiting and piracy appear to be growth industries." He also hit on a point that brought the issue close to home for even those uninvolved in global business:

> The cost of counterfeit and pirated products is not limited to lost revenue and jobs. Consumer health and safety is at stake, too. US Food and Drug Administration counterfeiting investigations have jumped from about five a year in the late 1990s to twenty-two in 2002. Viagra is known to be a frequent target of counterfeiters, but other commonly prescribed drugs such as Lipitor and Procrit are being targeted as well. Counterfeit drugs may contain too much,

too little, or none of a drug's active ingredient. Common every-day household products also are at risk. In December 2003, the Department of Homeland Security's Bureau of Immigration and Customs Enforcement announced seizures of electrical goods and batteries valued at approximately $8 million. Counterfeit batteries can explode in electronic equipment or children's toys. Even product approval marks certifying a product's safety are being counterfeited.

We all have a huge amount to gain from getting tough on IP theft. Curtailing the proliferation of counterfeit goods improves safety and raises quality levels across the board. Diminishing the potential loss of IP will lead many cautious entrepreneurs to expand into markets they now consider dangerous. Obviously, making sure that IP owners receive the income that is rightfully theirs also drives more money into our economy—money that adds jobs and raises the tax base. Just think what it would be possible to do with the hundreds of billions we're currently losing to people with no interest in our economy and no respect for our ingenuity.

## ALLOWING THE TENETS OF CONSCIENTIOUS EQUITY TO LEAD US TOWARD A SOLUTION

The core notion of Conscientious Equity is doing the right thing and giving everyone a stake in it. Elsewhere in this book, I have discussed how this principle benefits the hungry and the impoverished. Here, we need to look at how this concept aids the American entrepreneur. As I stated earlier in this chapter, American small and medium-sized businesses drive the creation of IP in this country. Yet they are especially susceptible to piracy because they don't have the resources to hire a team of lawyers to insure that their IP is safe. Huge corporations can spend tens of millions to acquire the best legal defense; the small-town inventor doesn't have the money to protect himself. We pay taxes to our government so it can protect us. Right now, it is not doing a very good job of protecting entrepreneurs.

Countries such as China, South Korea, and Japan have far fewer lawyers per capita than America does, but a much higher percentage of their lawyers work for their trade ministries than ours do. This helps these countries to enforce trade agreements they have negotiated—and to find ways around our laws. Governments in these nations employ a huge team of lawyers to protect their market and maximize the benefit of agreements they sign, including protecting their own IP.

The Import Administration and the Patent and Trademark Office, divisions of the U.S. Department of Commerce, are dedicated to enforcing our international commerce agreements and addressing IP theft. These departments are woefully understaffed. We need to invest in a dramatic increase in the legal personnel in these trade-enforcement groups, and we must give them the resources they need to deal with the enormity of the problem. We must charge them with the mission of finding who is responsible for the theft of our IP in China and elsewhere, and we need to give them the tools to combat it. We pay taxes to our government to protect us in precisely this way.

We must ensure that countries that steal from America will face the direst consequences—the withdrawal of access to the American market. Once we have documented evidence of foreign government complicity in the theft of American intellectual property, we can estimate the cost of that theft (for instance, the quarter of a trillion dollars we are losing in China) and not allow an amount of their products of equal value into our country. Such a response might seem extreme, and it would have its opponents within our borders (many American companies benefit from Chinese imports), but it is the only reasonable response by those charged to protect us against theft from American taxpayers.

If we are willing to be forceful, we can right an egregious wrong.

## CHAPTER SIX

# THE KIND OF FARM AID WILLIE NELSON NEVER IMAGINED

BONG DUMLAO AND HIS FAMILY LIVE ON A MOUNTAINTOP in the Philippines overlooking the South China Sea, where a brisk breeze supplies an endless stream of fresh air. The raspy sounds of the wind fluttering through the towering crown of a banyan tree and ruffling coconut fawns instill a strange, tenuous serenity.

Bong, his wife Clara, and their three children live in a one-room nipa hut—a bamboo frame held together by a thatched roof and walls made from the dried leaves of the ubiquitous nipa palm. The floor is smooth bamboo. Bong's hut, like most of its kind, is elevated a few feet off the ground. This creates natural convection, lowering the temperature by a handful of degrees and providing the family's only relief from grueling hot days and humid nights.

During the habagat season (June through November), the southwesterly monsoon arrives and the seas suddenly turn violent. During this time, Bong and his family huddle together for hours as torrential rains pummel them from every direction. The howling wind whisks through their hut, clawing at the filament and the few rusty nails that hold it together. As the storm rages, the terrified family members wonder if their hut will disintegrate, leaving them exposed to the savage elements.

To reach Bong's home, my colleagues and I drove my four-wheel-drive SUV several kilometers along gravel and dirt roads, until we reached a point where the monsoon rains had caused a massive mudslide to swallow up the road. Then, we walked for more than an hour along a winding dirt path up a steep mountainside.

Bong's hut has no running water, electricity, or any sort of plumbing. For fresh water, the family must walk more than a kilometer to a community well. Bong ekes out a living from a small plot of maize and coffee that he tends by hand, with the assistance of the crudest tools. He uses farming techniques that have not changed for several generations.

Clara is in her early twenties, but she looks much older. When I visited, she already had three young children and was pregnant with a fourth. Clara is barely 4 feet 10 inches tall. Nutritional deficiency stunts growth. Seeing her served as a reminder that the countries with the highest birth rates are often those least able to provide nourishment for their exploding populations.

As is customary, Bong offered us food soon after our arrival, with the friendly Filipino greeting "kain na" (let's eat). The only thing available for Clara to prepare was some rice that we flavored with vinegar and fiery hot chili peppers that Bong plucked from a bush nearby. Most days, Bong's family would have only one meal. Often, that meal would be rice, with perhaps some salt or ground coffee beans added for flavor. Before we ate, Bong said the Lord's Prayer. People all around the world have recited the words "Give us this day our daily bread" countless times. For the nine hundred million who experience extreme hunger each day—nearly fifteen percent of the world's inhabitants—these prayers go unanswered.

We ate with our hands and drank warm Coca-Cola. As we ate, Bong, eyes fixed downward, apologized for the few scoops of rice on our plates, even though this meal represented several days of food for his family. This broke my heart, especially because I knew that I could say nothing to assuage his sense of shame.

I could not stop looking at his children, who had no chance of receiving enough food to meet their most basic nutritional needs, let alone healthcare or a formal education. I'm not sure how many of them will even make it to adulthood.

Despite his long hours of hard work, Bong cannot compete even in his home area against the heavily subsidized producers of America and Europe. The old adage "Give a man a loaf of bread and you feed him for a day; teach him how to farm and you feed him for life" does not go far enough. You also must provide him a market. Because of the extreme tariffs levied on agricultural products by Japan and South Korea, Bong cannot export what he grows. His own government abandoned him by lowering tariffs and encouraging subsidized imports at the expense of family farmers like Bong. Meanwhile, because of large increases in food and energy prices, he and his loved ones—already on the verge of starvation—pay significantly more and receive less. What else can you take away from this family so that the already rich can continue to fill their coffers?

## A GOOD IDEA GONE BAD

One could say that the first law establishing agricultural subsidies in the United States was the Morrill Act of 1862, which provided federally controlled land for the creation of colleges that offered a heavy concentration in the agricultural sciences. The land-grant colleges, as these schools are known, are alive and well today, and include some of our most noted institutions, such as MIT, Cornell University, the University of Virginia, and the University of North Carolina. The Morrill Act provided federal money for the development of future farmers and farming techniques. The Hatch Act of 1887 extended this tactic by funding agricultural experiment stations in sixteen states that sought to improve farming and ranching techniques, advance agricultural technology, and solve problems endemic to the agricultural world. In 1914, the Smith-Lever Act provided additional support for agriculture education. All of these relatively small programs shored up the agricultural industry in this country through education, development, and research.

It wasn't until the Great Depression that the government started to offer cash subsidies directly to farmers. President Roosevelt's Agriculture Adjustment Act of 1933 offered crop insurance, price supports, import barriers, and other forms of aid to farmers who were barely earning enough to survive.[1] My father's family in West Virginia and my mother's family in Kentucky—both of which lived on small family farms—were very grateful for this help in their time of need. Helping farmers during this desperate era was noble and necessary, and it saved many lives and livelihoods.

Unfortunately, like most government-administered programs, agricultural subsidies have become grossly perverted, and they no longer serves the constituency for which they were designed. Fast-forwarding to the present, farmers make up a smaller percentage of the overall American population than they did in the 1930s, but they have a stronger voice in governmental policy. In large part, this is because they have done a very good job of aligning themselves with other powerful constituencies. A position paper written for the Cato Institute, a staunchly non-partisan advocacy group, notes that "farm-state legislators have co-opted the support of urban legislators, who seek increased subsidies in agriculture bills for programs such as food stamps. Legislators interested in rural environmental subsidies have also been co-opted as supporters of farm bills. Thus many legislators have an interest in increasing the USDA's budget, but there are few opposing them on behalf of the taxpayer."[2]

## A RECORD HARVEST OF PORK

Such thinking led to the 2008 Farm Bill. Over a five-year period, this bill offers three hundred billion dollars of agricultural subsidies and pork-barrel projects. When it landed on his desk, even President George W. Bush, who certainly showed a predilection for spending taxpayer money, felt obliged to veto the bill as containing too much pork and not enough bacon. Not to be spurned, Congress, with broad bipartisan support, overwhelmingly voted to override the President's veto.

One assumes that the president knew his veto had little chance of sticking. Despite the intense partisanship of Congress during the last years of the Bush administration, representatives had no trouble joining hands across the aisle when it came to these subsidies. They received a great deal of encouragement: the agriculture lobby spends more than a hundred million dollars each year to influence Congress. This is obviously an excellent investment, as that expenditure has netted twenty billion dollars per year in direct agricultural price subsidies. As if this weren't enough, the Farm Bill also subsidizes fertilizers, pesticides, and freight costs.

Most of us know and sympathize with the plight of poor American family farmers. Such farmers are at the mercy of unpredictable weather and uncontrollable price fluctuations. They often have a difficult time making a living. It is a misconception, however, to believe that farm subsidies exist to stabilize the incomes of farmers such as these. Eligibility for subsidies has nothing to do with low incomes or poverty reduction. Rather, it has to do with specific crops. Growers of corn, wheat, cotton, soybeans, and rice receive ninety percent of all farm subsidies. In total, only thirty-six percent of U.S. farm production is eligible for subsidy. These subsidies tend to go to large corporations and even wealthy individuals. The top ten percent of recipients receive seventy five percent of all federal agricultural subsidies. Recipients include the Fortune 500 companies International Paper, Kimberly Clark, Caterpillar, John Hancock, Mutual Life Insurance, Electronic Data Systems, and Chevron, which all invest in corporate farms.

Meanwhile, many wealthy celebrities receive payments from the government for *not* farming their land. Among those who have gotten such checks are Ted Turner, David Rockefeller, Scottie Pippen, and David Letterman (who reportedly gave his subsidy money to charity). According to an analysis of government records by the *Washington Post*, the government has paid at least 1.3 billion dollars in subsidies to people who do no farming at all.[3]

Congress did attempt to wean farmers off subsidies with the Federal Agriculture Improvement and Reform Act of 1996, better known as the "Freedom to Farm" law. The law offered farmers declining fixed "market transition payments" that protected farmers from market fluctuations. It also freed them to farm what they thought they could produce best, rather than the handful of crops for which they had previously received subsidies. The plan was for subsidies to total forty-seven billion dollars between 1996 and 2002 and drop precipitously after that. However, the Freedom to Farm law always had a significant number of detractors, and legislators worked away at the program nearly from the moment of its enactment. In total, the years from 1996 to 2002 saw subsidy payments of one hundred and twenty-one billion dollars, or more than two-and-a-half times the original projection.

The Farm Bill of 2002 did not even pretend to attempt to curtail subsidies. It added new subsidized crops and a new schedule of price guarantees, and it increased subsidy payments by nearly seventy-five percent. This set the stage for the Farm Bill of 2008 and its record-level largesse.

## A GAME WITH FEW WINNERS

Agricultural subsidies have become the largest corporate welfare program in the history of the United States. These subsidies have accomplished the complete opposite of their intended purpose. Ironically, the average income of farm households has greatly outpaced the growth of household incomes in other sectors since the Depression. Back in the thirties, farm household incomes were half the national average. In 2005, farm household incomes were twenty-six percent *higher* than the national average. Unfortunately, this wealth has not been spread around equally. The bulk of it goes to the mega-farmer, and the small family farmer continues to suffer.

Our tax dollars are helping continue this trend. Instead of saving the family farmer, who operates with the entrepreneurial spirit that has powered our economy for so long, subsidies provide capital for large corporations to buy out small farms and consolidate the industry.

The small farmer isn't the only one losing. Because subsidies protect some American farmers from foreign competition, they raise the cost of living for the rest of us. As the Cato report states, "The extensive federal welfare system for farm businesses is costly to taxpayers and creates distortions in markets. Subsidies induce farmers to overproduce, which pushes down prices and creates demands for further subsidies. Subsidies inflate land prices in rural America."[4] The Organization for Economic Co-operation and Development stated that, in 2004, the increase in domestic food prices caused by agricultural subsidies totaled more than sixteen billion dollars. This comes down to a cost of an additional hundred and forty-six dollars for the average American household, on top of what we are paying in taxes for subsidies.

And then there is the impact on the earth. "The distortions and perverse incentives of U.S. agricultural policies have encouraged practices that damage the environment" write authors Daniel Griswold, Stephen Slivinski, and Christopher Preble in a recent article for *Reason* magazine. They add:

> Trade barriers and subsidies stimulate production on marginal land, leading to overuse of pesticides, fertilizers, and other effluents. A central if unstated purpose of American farm policy is to promote production of commodities that would not be economical under competitive, free market conditions. This often means emphasizing crops better grown elsewhere, requiring more chemical assistance.
>
> Overuse of fertilizers and pesticides adds to runoff that pollutes rivers, lakes, and oceans. According to the World Resources Institute, agriculture is the biggest source of river and lake pollutants in the United States. A study by the Environmental Protection Agency found that 72 percent of US rivers and 56 percent of lakes it surveyed suffer from agriculture-related pollution. Areas of the Gulf of Mexico have become "dead zones" because of the runoff from farms in the Midwest. Even where fertilizers and pesticides are not used intensively, the mere act of plowing soil eliminates forest and grass cover, leaving soil exposed for weeks at a time and vulnerable to erosion. Erosion can build up silt in nearby rivers and downstream lakes.
>
> Domestic sugar protection has maintained a concentration of producers in central Florida who have used up water from the endangered Florida Everglades while spitting back phosphorous

content far above the level consistent with maintaining the surrounding ecosystem. The high runoff has seriously reduced periphyton, such as algae, that supports birds and other animal life. Congress has spent billions to repair the damage caused to the Everglades by the protected sugar industry.[5]

## SOWING SEEDS OF DISCONTENT AROUND THE WORLD

Agricultural subsidies are not only hurting us, they also have a negative impact on people around the world, as you can see in the story of Bong Dumlao. To better understand this impact, consider this: subsidized U.S. food products exported to Jamaica are cheaper than homegrown Jamaican crops. This makes it impossible for Jamaica's dirt-poor farmers to survive. If they cannot even compete in their own market, there is no way they can hope to export what they grow. Gripping poverty has the farmers stuck in a firm headlock, and American farm subsidies are to blame.

When the U.S. government guarantees American farmers a minimum payment for certain commodities, it encourages overproduction of these commodities. This drives down market prices, forces even higher subsidies—paid by taxpayer money, and creates surpluses that we then dump around the world, choking off local farmers in their home markets.

To make matters worse, as a condition of providing loans to developing countries to help them service their foreign debt, international lending agencies such as the International Monetary Fund (IMF) insist that developing countries keep their tariffs low. Low tariffs allow American agricultural exporters to sell millions of tons of food below the cost of production and wipe out local farmers' livelihoods.

This is not something we should take lightly or consider someone else's problem. In the same *Reason* article previously quoted, the authors address the effect of subsidies on citizens of the world and the dangers these subsidies pose for those of us at home:

> The frustration and despair caused by these policies undermine American security. Many people who depend on agriculture for their survival, both as a source of nourishment and a means of acquiring wealth, perceive U.S. farm policy as part of an anti-American narrative in which Washington wants to keep the rest of the world locked in poverty. Indeed, in a survey of anti-American sentiment around the world, the Pew Research Center found a majority of respondents in more than a dozen countries were convinced that U.S. farm and trade policies increased the "poverty gap" worldwide. These sentiments transcended geographic, ethnic, or religious boundaries. In such an environment, terrorist ringleaders find fertile ground for their message of hate and violence.
>
> Nicholas Stern, chief economist at the World Bank, is blunt about America's leadership role. "It is hypocritical to preach the advantages of free trade and free markets," Stern told the UN publication *Africa Recovery*, "and then erect obstacles in precisely those markets in which developing countries have a comparative advantage."[6]

## IT'S A COW'S LIFE

We are hardly the only guilty party. The EU pays out one hundred and thirty-three billion dollars in agricultural subsidies annually, with France being the main beneficiary. Remember, three billion people on this planet live on less than two dollars a day—yet a European cow receives more that that in subsidies. Meanwhile, Japan pays out forty-nine billion dollars a year in subsidies, and South Korea delivers twenty billion to its agricultural sector.

The developing nations are putting tremendous pressure to change these practices on the United States, the EU, Japan, and South Korea via the WTO, but their effort has little chance of making a significant impact. It certainly won't accomplish anything in the EU. French farmers have tremendous power. They can and will decimate the French economy if their leaders make any serious attempt to cut supports. Given the word to mobilize, French farmers will have their tractors at the gates of Paris, shutting down the city. No French politician has the guts to stand up to them.

It won't happen in Japan, either. Agricultural subsidies (approximately forty-four hundred dollars per acre of agricultural land, compared to three hundred dollars per acre in the EU and fifty dollars per acre in the United States) underwrite the Japanese political system. The Liberal Democratic Party (LDP) in Japan pays these subsidies to its core constituency, rural communities and farmers. Much of the money then is funneled back to LDP politicians as contributions and kickbacks. This system has allowed the LDP to monopolize political power in Japan for the past fifty years.

It is not going to happen in South Korea. Having worked closely with South Koreans for decades, I know that their radical farmers would actively and passionately work to bring down any South Korean politician who attempted to dismantle agricultural subsidies and tariffs. South Korean farmers were active participants in the WTO protests in Seattle and other parts of the world. They take their subsidies seriously and have no problem traveling around the globe to voice their opinions.

Many developing countries, including Bong's home country, the Philippines, have decided that it is cheaper to lower import tariffs and purchase subsidized food on the international market than to invest in farming infrastructure. However, this plan has backfired. Today, governments in Asia, Africa, and Latin America cannot find enough food to feed their people. Since January 2007, food prices have soared by as much as sixty percent, sparking riots in more than thirty countries.

## PUTTING DOLLARS IN THE RIGHT HANDS

As I mentioned earlier in this book, agricultural subsidies are a major sticking point in the Doha round of WTO negotiations. In the summer of 2008, in a last-ditch effort to move these talks along before the end of the Bush administration, the United States offered to cut its subsidy cap by three billion dollars. The developing WTO nations, led by Brazil and India, responded derisively, claiming that this cut still left U.S. subsidies higher than in 2007. Susan Schwab, then the U.S. Trade Representative, responded that, although this was true, the cut would cap the subsidy level below the amount of subsidies paid in seven of the previous ten years. In the end, this level of concession did nothing to move the talks along. The developing nations demanded that the United States drop the cap by an additional three billion dollars, even though they made no promises regarding the lower tariffs the United States and the EU sought in return.

In the end, pressure from the WTO isn't really the issue. The issue is that agricultural subsidies are bad for America, they are bad for the world, and it is time for us to end a practice that stopped doing what it was intended to do nearly seven decades ago. In 2006, the Congressional Budget Office concluded that "U.S. agriculture has more to gain from liberalization in terms of increased exports than it has to lose in terms of increased imports."[7] The report continues, "Subsidies tend to benefit the countries purchasing the subsidized products and to harm the countries granting the subsidies (although their agricultural sectors benefit)." The point is that greatly reducing our agricultural subsidies will create a more hospitable trade environment throughout the world. This will benefit all American exporters and could conceivably generate more income for our agricultural sector than that sector would be giving up in subsidies.

Whether mega-farmers and other corporations who have received the vast majority of subsidies would come out with a net gain is debatable. What is unquestionable, though, is that the American taxpayer would win big. We can refer to some models for precedents. In recent years, Argentina, Australia, and New Zealand have all done away with farm subsidies. Prior to the economic downturn in 2008 that affected nearly every sector of business worldwide, their agricultural industries were doing well.

The farm lobby is hugely powerful in the United States. We'd be more likely to convince corporate farmers to trade their tractors for dray horses than suffer the end of federal handouts. However, looking at agricultural subsidies through the prism of Conscientious Equity, one can only conclude that they are wrong and that they exclude far more people—even in their own sector—than they include. It is difficult to see how agricultural subsidies serve Americans, other than the mega-farmers, or anyone else around the world. They don't serve the labor community, which must be fuming over these payouts as factories close all over the country. They don't serve those of us who care about the environment, as huge farms receive incentives to employ techniques that degrade the land. They certainly don't serve the entrepreneurs who struggle without governmental aid to make a profit and employ as many people as possible.

The way we subsidize a certain class of our farmers hurts people all over the world and runs smack against the ideals that Americans claim to espouse. Such hypocrisy harms us and diminishes us. If we are truly going to embrace the tenets of Conscientious Equity, we need to revise this practice as soon as humanly possible. This will unquestionably be a struggle—a battle within our borders as tough as any in which we engage with a foreign nation to achieve

Conscientious Equity. It is, however, one we must choose to fight and must be determined to win. It is critical that we lead by example. An announcement that we are willing to stop doling out financial favors to the already rich will tell people like Bong Dumlao and their leaders that we are serious about making the world a more equitable place.

## CHAPTER SEVEN

# SANCTION FEVER

IN 432 B.C., THE ATHENIAN GENERAL Pericles banned the mer-
chants of the city of Megara from the harbors and marketplaces
of Athens. The ban, known as the Megaran Decree, was enacted
because Megaran citizens allegedly cultivated land consecrated to
Demeter, the Greek goddess of the earth. Pericles intended the
ban to strangle the Megaran economy as punishment for the city's
blasphemy. Instead, it drove Megara to seek the aid of Sparta and
helped launch the Peloponnesian War—a conflict that, ultimately,
diminished the great Athenian Empire.

The Megaran Decree is the earliest known instance of a unilateral
trade sanction, although there are some indications that the practice
took place during wartime in the ancient Near East.[1] As has been the

case with so many trade sanctions in the two-and-a-half millennia since the Megaran Decree, it didn't work out at all as intended.

## THOSE WHO DO NOT LEARN FROM HISTORY

In 1807, President Thomas Jefferson imposed a unilateral trade embargo on Britain in response to its attack on the American ship the *USS Chesapeake*. The embargo had only a modest impact on British exports, but it managed to devastate the economy of New England, severely handicap the entire American shipping industry, and lead a whole class of American entrepreneurs to become expert smugglers.[2]

In 1938, in response to the Panay Incident, in which Japanese warplanes sank the *USS Panay*, President Franklin Roosevelt instituted the first of a series of sanctions against Japan.[3] What started with the president discouraging the shipment of goods and the extension of credit to Japan grew into a mandatory embargo against shipping military supplies to that country and, ultimately, to the freezing of all Japanese assets in the United States. This last move had the direct effect of shutting off all trade between the two nations, including trade in oil, at a time when Japan imported eighty percent of its oil from America. In order to keep the imperialistic Japanese war machine running, the country invaded the Dutch East Indies to commandeer its oil—and launched the attack on Pearl Harbor (and the simultaneous invasion of the Philippines, where America had military bases) that changed the course of American history.

Although the lessons of the past vividly show that unilateral trade sanctions have little chance of success, our leaders have been stunningly slow to absorb this message. In fact, all indications are that we have not learned this lesson at all. We have levied more than half of the sanctions we have exercised in the course of our history *in the last ten years*. In the last half-century, we have sanctioned Cuba for its commitment to Communism, Iran for its support of terrorism, Sudan for its human rights violations, North Korea for its development of nuclear weapons, and many more countries for many other reasons. We literally have sanctioned everywhere from Angola (for the illegal sale of diamonds) to Zimbabwe (for politically motivated violence).

During the Cold War, we employed the exact opposite of the massive aid and lopsided trade that we graciously bestowed on Western Europe and Japan via the Marshall Plan, on the Soviet Union and its Communist bloc cronies. American export regulators worked overtime to deny our Communist adversaries any sort of trade, finance, or technology. At the start, these sanctions had an impact because Western Europe, Japan, and Canada were equally committed to the strict enforcement of similar sanctions. However, such multilateralism faded fast. By the mid-sixties, our allies began relaxing their export controls. Ultimately, the Soviets were able to import everything they needed from enthusiastic trading partners who happened to be our political allies, and we had growing levels of unemployment.

When I think of our sanction history with the USSR, a classic example comes to mind. President Jimmy Carter, in response to the Soviet Union's actions in Poland, sanctioned the supply of goods and services required to build the Soviet pipeline for which the American company Caterpillar had a huge contract to provide heavy equipment. The embargo immediately terminated Caterpillar's Soviet business. Komatsu of Japan quickly stepped in, and construction of the pipeline finished under budget and on time. The upshot was twelve thousand worker-years shifting from Illinois to Tokyo. Komatsu was able to strengthen its company and compete more fiercely with Caterpillar in Europe, Latin America, and the Middle East. Meanwhile, Poland continued to suffer as a Soviet satellite until the end of the Cold War.

## PLAYING A LOSING GAME

Embargoes and trade sanctions are anathema to the concept of Conscientious Equity. Whereas Conscientious Equity espouses the use of international commerce to raise the prospects of all people, American unilateral sanctions are a particularly boorish example of our country throwing around its weight. In many cases, these sanctions make us look like bullies. In still more, they make us look terribly out of touch.

Trade sanctions rarely have the anticipated effect on our adversaries. Usually, they hurt only American manufacturers and workers. We have eager European and Asian competitors tripping over themselves to fill every purchase order and contract from which we walk away. Although it is difficult to quantify, some estimates suggest that sanctions cost American entrepreneurs at least seventy billion dollars in lost sales annually. This translates into six hundred thousand jobs. The real cost is exponentially larger, however, as organizations in many countries consider us to be erratic as a supply source and beholden to an impulsive Congress. These organizations, therefore, choose to send their business elsewhere, even during the times when we are free to trade with them. The dwindling number of countries we have never sanctioned feel a similar level of skittishness. It is impossible to calculate how much money we have lost because our foreign counterparts wonder when the American sanction hammer will come down on them, but I have witnessed their nervousness first-hand.

Today, we use trade sanctions as a way to show disdain without sending in the Marines. We sanction to protect the environment, to protest military action, to improve treatment of labor, for drug trafficking, for money laundering, and, ironically, for having restrictive trade policies. In fact, if we consistently applied our positions, we would only have a handful of countries with which we could do business.

This has landed us in a disheartening place. Publicly, friendly governments scorn our trade embargoes and sanctions as morally wrong—even likening our policies to a form of "trade terrorism"— and childishly naive. In private, they relish the good fortune of not having to contend with American competitors in dozens of markets.

I do not believe that the causes underlying these sanctions are frivolous. Of course, all good people support human rights and don't want dangerous weapons in the hands of those who would use them indiscriminately. However, our sanctions are completely out of control. More important, they accomplish virtually nothing but to strip jobs from and effectively reduce the wages of hundreds of thousands of Americans. Unless sanctions are airtight and multilateral, they have absolutely no chance to succeed.

I am hardly alone in this assessment. In a white paper from the Peterson Institute for International Economics (a Washington-based think tank) titled "U.S. Economic Sanctions: Their Impact on Trade, Jobs, and Wages," the authors note:

> Most of the analysis of the effectiveness of economic sanctions suggests they have limited utility for changing the behavior or governments of target countries. Previous research at the Institute for International Economics concluded that US sanctions had positive outcomes in fewer than one in five cases in the 1970s and 1980s.
>
> In addition to the immediate impact of sanctions on trade with the target, many American businessmen claim that the effects of even limited unilateral US sanctions go well beyond targeted sectors. They also argue that the effects linger long after they are lifted because US firms come to be regarded as "unreliable suppliers." Sanctioned countries may avoid buying from US exporters even when sanctions are not in place, thus giving firms in other countries a competitive advantage in those markets.
>
> Exports lost today may mean lower exports after sanctions are lifted because US firms will not be able to supply replacement parts or related technologies. Foreign firms may also design US intermediate goods and technology out of their final products for fear of one day being caught up in a US sanction episode.[4]

The Cato Institute's position on trade sanctions is strikingly similar to that of the Peterson Institute for International Economics:

> From Cuba to Iran to Burma, sanctions have failed to achieve the goal of changing the behavior or the nature of target regimes. Sanctions have managed only to deprive American companies of investment opportunities and market share and to punish domestic consumers, while hurting the poor and most vulnerable in the target countries.
>
> As well as inflicting economic damage, sanctions have been a foreign policy flop.... For example, the Nuclear Proliferation Act of 1994 failed to deter India and Pakistan from testing nuclear weapons in May of 1998. Sanctions have utterly failed to change the nature or basic behavior of governments in Cuba, Burma, Iran, Nigeria, Yugoslavia, and a number of other target countries.

In the handbook it prepared for the One Hundred Seventh Congress, Cato took these thoughts further:

> Trade sanctions seldom work because of the competitive global marketplace and the nature of regimes most likely to arouse America's ire. Although the United States is by far the world's largest economy, its global economic leverage is limited. The United States accounts for only thirteen percent of the world's merchandise exports and sixteen percent of its imports. If Washington seeks to punish another country by unilaterally withholding exports, such as farm products, computers, or oil-drilling services, other global suppliers stand ready to fill the gap. Even if sanctions inflict some pain on the target country, they typically fail because of the nature of the regimes most likely to become targets of sanctions. Human rights abuses tend to vary inversely with economic development. Governments that systematically deprive citizens of basic human rights typically intervene in daily economic life, resulting in underdeveloped and relatively closed economies. Such nations are the least sensitive to economic pressure. The autocratic nature

of their governments also means that they are relatively insulated from any domestic discontent caused by sanctions. If anything, sanctions tend to concentrate economic power in the hands of the target government and reduce that of citizens.[5]

The handbook underscores its point with some cogent examples. The American embargo against Cuba, for example, has done nothing to loosen Castro's hold on that nation or to improve conditions for the Cuban people. Meanwhile, American companies, which once did robust business in Cuba, have lost nearly a half a century of sales. A visit to Cuba even led Pope John Paul II to denounce sanctions.

In the late 1990s, President Clinton and the Republican Congress imposed severe sanctions on Burma for its political extremism. The sanctions failed to effect regime change. According to Cato, "The only result has been to push the people of Burma deeper into poverty and deprive them of the beneficial effects of engagement with American companies."

These examples identify another problem with sanctions: they rob the people they intend to help of access to the model of the American entrepreneurial effort. This is especially problematic in the developing world. There, despotic governments feel few of the effects of American sanctions, as they derive their money from illegitimate sources and rule with such an iron fist that the ire of their people is meaningless. Meanwhile, the citizens, who have much to gain from exposure to the American example, have no way to pull themselves up by their bootstraps.

I believe this is especially true for Cuba. Being so close to our borders, it is a natural trading partner. In addition, we share a close affinity with the Cuban people, as evidenced by the large and vibrant Cuban populations in America and the affection for American goods and popular culture that exists on that island nation even under the Castro regime. In fact, before Castro came to power, there was considerable talk of Cuba becoming the fifty-first state. One wonders how different Cuba might have been politically if, rather than isolating Cubans from our goods and services for the past fifty years, we continued to do business with them freely, exposing them continuously to our entrepreneurial spirit (we have chosen this path so far with Venezuela, so it is not inconceivable for us to stay open for business with a nation run by an extreme left-wing ruler). It is difficult for me to believe that Cuba would have taken its lead from distant Russia for so long (and now China and Iran) if we had treated our neighbors differently.

Of course, the embargo does not mean that there is no business being done in Cuba with American products. If you were to go to Cuba, visit its shops and restaurants, and walk down its streets, you would see a number of American items. You'd find Chevys from the fifties and sixties cruising down Cuban roads. However, Americans are not the ones supplying these cars or the replacement parts for them. Rather, they come from Canada or Mexico. American businesses ship a good deal of product to Merida, in the Yucatan—much more than this city (or even the region) could possibly use. The reason is that Merida is very close to Cuba. Because of our sanctions, and because there is a demand for American products within this sanctioned nation, intermediaries ship our goods into that country, adding their margins on top of ours. This prevents Americans from selling products directly at a price that more Cubans could afford and, therefore, suppresses what would otherwise be an extremely active market.

This example tells us that our sanctions aren't doing much to deprive the Cuban people or punish its leadership. It also tells us that both Cubans and American entrepreneurs would be much better off if we simply acknowledged that fifty years of sanctions have gained us very little politically. If Cuba becomes a more open society soon (as many suspect), it probably won't be because it finally bent from the lack of access to fairly priced Coca-Cola. It will happen because Communism has run its course on that island so close to our shores, which might have happened much sooner if our entrepreneurs had been visiting regularly and openly. When Cuba does become more open, the warehouses of South Florida will be bulging with products made in America on their way to Cuba, and Miami will be booming with the financial activity of rebuilding that nation.

## CURING OURSELVES OF SANCTION FEVER

The only people who seem to believe that trade sanctions have any political value are the politicians that dole them out so freely. Why do they continue to employ this tool with such regularity when it is so abundantly clear that sanctions rarely work? Part of the reason is political convenience. It is simply easier to slap a sanction on a country that doesn't act in a way that meets our standards than to dig deeper and employ the diplomacy and incentives that address these problems at their roots.

The rest is ignorance. The simple fact is that our leaders—including those who make decisions that have a profound impact on how we do business around the world—are woefully undereducated with regard to international commerce and the value of such commerce in spreading the American example. I will discuss at length in the next chapter why we should demand that our government representatives better understand what they're talking and legislating about concerning our business with other countries. For now, suffice it to say that we haven't held our elected officials to the highest standards in this area and that, as a result, we have paid a steep price.

Still, regardless of the cause, Congress is burning up with sanction fever—and the rest of us are suffering the symptoms. The first thing we need to do is take a step back and radically rethink our attitude toward sanctions. If we ever choose to use them, we should weigh doing so carefully and target them primarily against rogue countries with out-of-control weapons programs. Making it more difficult for dangerous regimes to build lethal weapons is eminently sensible and a necessary part of our national security, as is punishing those regimes for accessing the materials for weapons of mass destruction on the black market. However, such sanctions have teeth only if we make them in concert with other suppliers around the world. Multilateral sanctions are often extremely effective, because they have true punitive effect. We must seek the compliance of the world's other major economies before we levy any sanctions. Doing anything on our own, as I'm sure is clear to you now, is tantamount to doing nothing.

In nearly every case, a better policy than sanctions is to let American entrepreneurs freely export and travel abroad, taking with them our values, our culture, and our ideas. This might not make for the dramatic grandstanding on C-SPAN that face-time-hungry politicians seem to so richly desire, but it offers the only long-term opportunity to spread our way of life. As recent experience has taught us, it is virtually impossible to force our values on other cultures. Doing so is utterly inconsistent with the precepts of Conscientious Equity. Longer-view experience has also taught us, however, that, when we give people from other parts of the world access to the American spirit via our products, our ingenuity, and our ideas, they only want more—and such exports allow people to embrace the concept of Conscientious Equity in ways harmonious to their cultures. We can see successful examples in Japan, Germany, South Korea, and any number of other nations around the world.

We don't need sanctions to influence the world and teach our ideals. We just need to extend the reach of our people as far as possible. By allowing Americans to engage with the world in open commerce, the only losers will be tyranny, poverty, and ignorance.

## CHAPTER EIGHT

# A LITTLE KNOWLEDGE MAKES A DANGEROUS LEADER

I VIVIDLY REMEMBER ARRIVING at Bogotá's El Dorado International Airport in the mid 1990s, clearing immigration, and heading toward the city. I was decidedly on edge, knowing that I was entering a land with one of the highest homicide and kidnapping rates in the world. For an American entrepreneur, Bogotá was a notoriously dangerous place to be.

Violence had been rocking Colombia for decades, and tension permeated the thin Andean air. Nearly every Colombian family had been tragically touched by terror, murder, and kidnapping. During the period when I first visited, Colombia was the nexus of ruthless drug lords with unfathomable financial resources controlled by a relentless Marxist-Leninist group known as FARC (Revolutionary Armed Forces of Colombia or in Spanish, from which it gets its acronym, *Fuerzas Armadas Revolutionaries de Colombia*). FARC had long been designated an international terrorist organization because its leaders had ordered the taking of the lives of tens of thousands of innocent civilians.

One of FARC's victims was the father of former Colombian president, Alvaro Uribe. The organization killed the elder Uribe during an attempted kidnapping in 1983. President Uribe took office in 2002 and was re-elected to a second term in 2006. Since he has been president, the homicide rate in Bogotá is down seventy-one percent. Although still dangerous, it is now a safer city than, among others, Detroit, Baltimore, St. Louis, Caracas, Rio, and Mexico City. During this same period, FARC has become dramatically weaker, down from sixteen thousand guerillas in 2001 to eight thousand in 2008. This is impressive progress, which you can sense when visiting Bogotá today.

However, it will take a long time for Colombians to rid themselves of their deeply imprinted fear. To avoid attention, wealthy businesspeople drive to five-star restaurants in older Japanese cars. For the same reason, the restaurants have subdued lighting on the outside. Offices in Bogotá rarely have signs or fancy storefronts. The face they present to the public is one of rundown warehouses—warehouses that just happen to house businesses that are among the most sophisticated and best managed in Latin America. Bogotá is a city not of glitz and glamour but of quiet resolve and determination.

Under President Uribe, Colombia became a much friendlier place for foreign entrepreneurs. Realizing this, the U.S. Trade Representative initiated negotiations in the spring of 2004 for a free trade agreement between our countries. The negotiations led

to a pact that would immediately eliminate duties on eighty percent of American products shipped into Colombia and phase out
the remaining duties over a ten-year period. The agreement also
included significant concessions from Colombia regarding intellectual property. Because more than ninety percent of Colombian
products already enter the United States duty-free, this was a considerable win for America. The Colombian agreement is our best
to date, one that comes closest to the ideals I am suggesting we
implement with Conscientious Equity Accords, with the most comprehensive language ever written into a trade agreement on labor
rights, environmental protections, and intellectual property rights.
Colombia, though not an enormous market, is home to forty-five
million people. In 2008, we did twenty-four billion dollars in trade
with Colombia, but we ran a deficit of more than a billion and a half
dollars. As we have learned, free trade agreements with countries of
this size can have an immediate positive impact, both in reversing
our deficit and in the amount of trade we do with that country. A
Colombian importer told me that his business with America would
increase by forty percent as soon as we had an FTA in place.

After both governments signed the agreement, President Bush
submitted it to Congress for an up-or-down vote. Congress had
ninety legislative days to hold this vote, as required by the "fast-
track" authority under which we negotiated the deal. Since 1974,
every presidential administration has had Congress vote on its
trade agreements this way.

This time, though, it didn't happen. In what was both an example of the worst of partisan politics and an indication of how little
our elected officials understand international commerce, Speaker
of the House Nancy Pelosi made an *ex post facto* change to House
rules to avoid the required vote, withdrawing from the timetable
and, thus, relegating the Colombian deal—an FTA that is good
for American business—to permanent limbo. Congress, until now,
has never voted down a trade agreement negotiated by a sitting

president from either party. Speaker Pelosi, however, dismantled the only process that allows any administration to conduct good-faith negotiations with foreign nations. No one is going to take the United States at its word if Congress changes the rules in the middle of the game.

Let's consider the purely commercial reasons why this deal should have passed with overwhelming bipartisan support. Colombia has enjoyed preferential-trade access to the U.S. market for the past eighteen years as part of the Andean Trade Preferences Act (ATPA). ATPA was created to provide farmers and workers in this area with alternatives to being swallowed up by the narcotics industry that is omnipresent throughout the Andean region. As a result, ninety-three percent of Colombian exports arrive in the United States duty-free. Colombia wants the FTA because it would both make this preferential trade access permanent and solidify Colombia's commitment to democracy and economic freedom. The last time ATPA came before Congress for renewal, in June of 2007, it passed with an overwhelming majority of three hundred and sixty-five votes.

Meanwhile, tariffs ranging from seven to eighty percent currently apply to U.S. products exported to Colombia, putting American exporters at a significant disadvantage. The U.S.-Colombia Free Trade Agreement levels the playing field by providing much greater benefits to American exporters than it gives to Colombia, whose products already arrive in the United States with very few restrictions. An illustration of how this FTA would work to our advantage is flowers. Right now, flowers that Colombia exports to the United States arrive here duty-free, whereas the tractors and fertilizers we send to Colombia to help grow these flowers pay substantial duties. Under the FTA, the equipment we send to Colombia would also go in duty-free.[1]

Therefore, if this agreement simply gives American exporters access to a market that Colombian exporters already have, even as it protects labor leaders, defends unions, sets safety standards, protects the environment, secures our intellectual property, and instills due process (all important components of the agreement), why didn't it pass instantly? The answer, sadly, is partisan politics and grandstanding against an unpopular president.

Partisan politics are, unfortunately, a fact of political life that seem unlikely to change in the conceivable future, even with a different president in office and a different political party in control of Congress. Much good legislation dies this way, and we should consider this shameful, even as we acknowledge the realities. Our leaders' level of ignorance regarding the business we do overseas—and the state of the world in general—however, is something we must demand they rectify. We don't have the luxury of allowing our politicians to continue to be this badly informed.

## I WANT A NEW DRUG

Our leaders' lack of understanding of essential economic concepts is hardly limited to international commerce. Earlier in this book, I discussed the Nixon Shock, when President Nixon took the United States off the gold standard. This shock put our economy in a precarious place, never more so than today.

Take a moment to reflect on the developing countries that have debased their currencies through deficit spending over the past twenty years. Argentina, Brazil, Egypt, Indonesia, the Philippines, Russia, Venezuela...the list goes on and on. What this does to the citizens of these countries is unconscionable. They work their entire lives and save whatever they can. Over time, they accumulate enough to retire. They look forward to some years of tranquility. Then—poof—some corrupt, greedy leader turns on the printing presses, and their entire life's savings are devalued to the point where they spend what should have been retirement years struggling for survival, with no time to recover their losses.

The American printing presses have never worked as hard as they are working today. Our 2009 budget deficit, as calculated by the nonpartisan Congressional Budget Office (CBO), is estimated to be 1.85 trillion dollars, out of a record-breaking federal budget of 4 trillion dollars. For every dollar that we collect in taxes, we spend two. The CBO further projects a budget deficit from 2010–2019 of 9.3 trillion dollars on top of that 1.85 trillion-dollar figure. Our current national debt is 11 trillion dollars. Based on these calculations, we would be doubling it in only ten years.

Shockingly, this is the good news. The situation is likely to be considerably worse. The CBO offered this number as a best-case scenario based on current spending, overly optimistic economic growth projections, and higher tax collections. An inevitable increase in tax rates will assuredly result in a lower tax base as business declines, American companies move offshore, and jobs disappear. Our current deficit is so monumental that we can cover it only by borrowing or printing dollars. Even the Chinese don't have enough dollars to invest to shore up our deficits—assuming they even wanted to do so.

Why do we believe that we are any different from the reckless governments I mentioned earlier that trashed their countries through printing-press economic policies? Why does an electrician in New York City make fifty dollars an hour while the same tradesman in Mexico City makes fifty *cents* an hour? Do we believe that the American standard of living is our birthright no matter how badly we manage our economic and international trade interests? The U.S. dollar will never be the same. American workers put their faith in "In God We Trust." Yet millions of Americans reaching retirement age will be devastated to learn that they may fare no better than those in other countries whose leaders debased their currencies and drove them into poverty.

Ironically, even the "printing presses" are an invention. Many Americans mistakenly believe that the trillions of dollars that pay for the unprecedented level of recent government intervention, entitlements, and social welfare are securely stashed away in a big safe somewhere in Washington. In reality, there is no vault and there is no cash. This money is nothing more than a series of keystrokes on a computer—"vapor paper" made of nothing but thin air.

Quantitative easing is a phrase that has come into the lexicon lately. When interest rates are at or near zero and commercial banks are still not lending money, the Fed injects massive amounts of money into the economy through accounts held by the banks at the Federal Reserve. The Fed buys bank securities (loan portfolios, mortgages, toxic assets, etc.). "Quantitative" means infusing a large quantity of money; "easing" means making it easy to access these funds. However, with nothing actually easing these funds, the problems compound.

To fund the federal budget deficit over the next decade, the Fed must sell a mind-numbing amount of debt, which it auctions off to investors and even foreign governments. This is only the beginning of the consequences of government spending run amok. The sheer amount of debt is so monumental that there will not be enough buyers at the Treasury auctions to absorb it. The Fed will be forced to buy its own "paper."

In private business, you would go to jail for this.

The U.S. government seems to think it can solve our debt problem by creating more debt. Monetizing government debt is what Third World countries do. Today in Zimbabwe, for example, the government has printed so much money that the smallest denomination bill you can own is 1 billion dollars. That is just enough to buy a single loaf of bread.

China, the largest buyer of U.S. treasury bills, has already fired a shot across our bow. The People's Central Bank of China recently announced, "Policy mistakes made by some central banks may bring inflation to the whole world," and "major currency devaluations may arise."[2] The announcement refers to quantitative easing, and China is clearly worried its large holdings of U.S. dollars and treasury bills will lose their value. The scary thing is that China may be right.

This is a particularly dangerous case of our politicians making terrifying decisions based on limited understanding. Let's dig a little deeper. In economics, the total amount of money available at any point in time is known as the money supply. M1 tracks the most liquid form of money: the currency in circulation including checking accounts. Presently, our M1 money supply is approximately 1.6 trillion dollars. M2 is M1 plus saving deposits and time deposits of less than one hundred thousand dollars. Our current M2 money supply is 8.3 trillion dollars. M3 tells the true story, though. M3 is M1 plus M2 plus large deposits, institutional funds, U.S. government funds and reserves, Eurodollars (U.S. dollars held overseas by foreign banks and governments), and U.S. treasury bills. The current M3 money supply is estimated at sixteen trillion dollars.

In March 2006, the Federal Reserve ceased to publish the M3 monetary aggregate because the "cost to collecting the underlying data and publishing M3 outweigh the benefits."[3] This is an obvious case of obfuscation. The real reason the Fed stopped publishing M3 is that the twenty percent annual growth in money supply is completely out of control. And that's before we factor in the next eleven trillion dollars of debt.

There is convincing empirical evidence that the rate of inflation is tied directly to the growth of the money supply. In other words, you cannot simply turn on the allegorical printing presses without ominous consequences. If dollars were as available as sand on the beach, how valuable would they be? The more you have of something, the less it is worth. I know this and you know this. I assume our politicians know it as well, but they aren't acting as though they do. A devalued currency reduces buying power as inflation soars. Therefore, in a sense, our government is stealing from you every time it creates more "vapor paper."

I wear a 1930 twenty-dollar Double Eagle gold coin around my neck as a symbol of our great country. It is nearly one ounce of twenty-two carat gold. When President Nixon took the United States off the gold standard, the coverage of gold bullion to our paper money had slipped from one hundred percent in 1933 to twenty-five percent. Today it is less than *one and a half percent*. Meanwhile, my Double Eagle twenty-dollar piece is worth more than a thousand dollars.

The four-trillion-dollar 2009 federal budget is equivalent to roughly eighty percent of all the gold that was ever mined in the history of the world.

In the late eighteenth century, low demand for British goods in China and high demand for Chinese goods such as silk and tea in Britain forced the British traders to purchase these products with silver and gold, the only currency accepted by the Chinese. The British quickly began accumulating a large trade deficit that they could not sustain. They needed to find an economic substitute for the silver and gold that would come with greatly reduced prices. The solution, although illegal, was to begin smuggling opium into China from the plentiful poppy fields of the Indo-Gangetic plain. Despite Emperor Qing's prohibition of the import of opium into China, it wasn't long before many Chinese people, including government officials, became addicted to the opium.

Raw opium contains some twenty different alkaloids, of which morphine is one. Morphine affects the central nervous system. It also impairs mental and physical performance, relieves fear and anxiety, and produces euphoria. Morphine's euphoric effect is highly addictive. Tolerance (the need for higher and higher doses to maintain the same effect) and physical and physiological dependence develop quickly. The malevolent outcome of morphine addiction is that it masks any underlying health problems, so, although a user may actually be dying, the euphoria deadens the pain until the person succumbs to the disease.

China's addiction to opium ultimately led to two Opium Wars with the British Empire—from 1839 to 1842 and from 1856 to 1860. China was routed and disgraced both times. Britain forced the Treaty of Nanjing and the Treaty of Tianjin on the now-feeble China. Together, these are commonly known as "the Unequal Treaties." The British gained extraterritorial rights, including its settlement in Shanghai and the cession of Hong Kong Island, from which they could freely operate trading activities, including the unrestricted importation of opium.

Several other countries, including France, Germany, Russia, and Japan, demanded and received similar arrangements from China. The humiliation of the Unequal Treaties eventually led to the fall of the Qing Dynasty in 1912 and, ultimately, the end of dynastic rule. In just forty years, China had fallen from one of the greatest empires ever assembled to lying prostrate before hated foreigners. It is one of the most rapid declines of any empire in the history of world and can be largely attributed to the opium that caused China to surrender its dignity and pride.

China's addiction erased centuries of glory and unleashed a thirty-year revolution. It allowed for events such as the Rape of Nanjing, the communist takeover in 1949, and the purges of the Cultural Revolution to take place. By its end, it created conditions in which China's citizens in several cities lived under foreign sovereignty within their own country.

You could say that China's downfall could be attributed to morphine economics. If you study China's sad history throughout the nineteenth and twentieth centuries, you can certainly understand its distrust of the West. China has passed through decades that no great nation should ever have to tolerate.

China's addiction should have served as a cold, stark warning. Imagine if we ever became addicted to something as devastating as opium. What would America's fate be if we lay helpless and paralyzed before the world? Would the outcome be any less wicked than the Unequal Treaties?

Although morphine economics ended in China, another nation fell under its deadly spell: the United States of America. As its economy eroded in the past decade, the United States began accumulating mountains of debt. This debt has become our morphine. We borrow money to pay debts today, unfazed by the legacy of the debt that we will face down the road. The euphoria of appearing to have the economy under control masks the worthless "vapor paper" currency that is being printed to stave off an economic collapse.

There are those among us who believe that out-of-control spending will make us healthy. They will look at any glimmer of improvement and shout out that the trillions we are spending (money we don't have, by the way) are having a positive impact. Do not be fooled. We are becoming weaker. Any euphoria anyone is feeling is only the work of a sinister drug.

The ultimate irony, of course, is that whereas the United States is being crushed by its runaway debt, this debt is being bought up by China—a nation that innately understands the perils of morphine economics. I think Emperor Qianlong, wherever he rests with his ancestors, gets no satisfaction from seeing a mighty nation make the same mistakes he did. It is up to us to learn the lesson and reverse our dependence on morphine economics before it causes irreparable damage to the economic health of our country and that of our future generations.

There is, of course, a way out. The question is whether our elected officials have the know-how and tenacity to lead us there. Recent history suggests that the answer isn't encouraging. This is one of the strongest reasons why we need to get everyone in our government thinking about Conscientious Equity right away.

## SO MANY POLITICIANS, SO LITTLE
## UNDERSTANDING OF INTERNATIONAL
## COMMERCE

During a recent trip up to Capitol Hill to advocate for the
U.S.-Colombian Free Trade Agreement, I visited the offices of
Congressman Gregory Meeks (D-NY). Congressman Meeks represents New York's Sixth Congressional District. The district covers southeast Queens and includes at its heart John F. Kennedy
(JFK) International Airport. Congressman Meeks is a member of
the Congressional Black Caucus and the Democratic Leadership
Council. Unlike most of his colleagues in his party, Congressman
Meeks supports our pending FTAs. He impressed me with
his knowledge of complex trade issues; he understands increased
overseas business, and travel is extremely important to his
district. More trade means more jobs for his constituents at JFK
Airport.

I questioned the congressman about why his party is so adamantly opposed to the Colombian agreement. It is one thing for
politicians not to understand international commerce, which we
can remedy by working harder to educate them. However, to misunderstand the political ramifications of rejection for partners
like President Uribe and Juan Manuel Santos, the man who followed him in the presidency in a landslide victory and who very
strongly shares his pro-American views, is to misunderstand that
such rejection hands Hugo Chavez an incredible political gift next
door in Venezuela. If our trade situation with Colombia worsens
(the United States is currently Colombia's leading trading partner), this will destabilize the Colombian economy and make the
government easy prey for an extreme leftist like Chavez. Allowing
this to happen when we can prevent it and help ourselves at the
same time—the very foundation of Conscientious Equity—is
unforgivable.

The Colombian people loved Uribe and they love Santos. They changed their constitution to allow Uribe to run for a second term as president, and more than five million Colombians signed a petition for his eligibility to run for a third term. When the Colombian courts rejected this, the Colombian people turned to Santos because they were convinced that he would continue Uribe's policies—policies that they believe represent all Colombians. They believe Santos will maintain a strong alliance with the United States and continue to avoid the influence of Hugo Chavez.

I proposed to Congressman Meeks that the comparison between Uribe (who was still president when Meeks and I met) and Colombia, and Chavez and Venezuela is, next to South Korea and North Korea, the most glaring illustration of good versus evil in the world today. The congressman agreed and then told me something that caused my jaw to drop: many people in his party do not see it that way. They don't necessarily think that Chavez's actions are wrong. They saw Uribe as someone who allowed assassins to target union leaders. A September 2008 letter to Uribe from U.S. Representative George Miller, the chair of the House Education and Labor Committee, confirms this. In the letter, Miller tells Uribe, "Our two ally nations should work together to help Colombia improve its labor laws, decrease the ongoing violence, and finally put an end to the impunity enjoyed by those who have perpetrated thousands of anti-labor killings. These challenges have taken on heightened significance this year as the violence in Colombia has escalated over 2007 levels."[4]

This argument simply doesn't hold true. For decades, Colombia has been a violent place for all of its citizens. We have seen, however, that this violence is decreasing. Meanwhile, there is little to suggest that labor leaders experience any more violence than an average citizen does. In fact, a number of Colombians close to the situation have told me that labor leaders regularly target management for harm, rather than the reverse. They have told me that the threat against those who run businesses is at least as strong as it is against those who organize unions of workers in those businesses.

Since Uribe came to office, violence against everyone—including labor leaders—has declined significantly. Connecting him with this violence is not only wrong; it is also irresponsible.

## DISPELLING THE MYTHS

By this point in this book, I've laid out for you what I hope is a persuasive argument for the value of Conscientious Equity Accords with all of our trading partners. In my mind, this is the ultimate win-win situation. Conscientious Equity Accords allow us to spread the American message in a non-threatening way, to regulate for our greatest social concerns, to generate greater income for American-based exporters, and—as we have seen in nearly every case in which we have signed the less comprehensive FTAs that we have used to date—to boost the economies of our trading partners, as well. The only losers in a world driven by open international commerce are the corrupt and the despotic. Yet, with great regularity, our elected officials vote against the kind of business that lies at the heart of such an accord.

According to the Cato Institute's Center for Trade Policy Studies, members of the One Hundred Tenth Congress (the session that served in 2007 and 2008) voted against free trade fifty-eight percent of the time (I'm using the term "free trade" here because Cato used that term. My feeling is that politicking from both sides of the argument has so encumbered this term that it has lost its meaning). Certainly, Democrats are less open to the vigorous promotion of international commerce; they voted against it sixty-six percent of the time. But Republicans just barely come out in favor, voting against free trade forty-nine percent of the time.[5]

Obviously, these people see the prospects and possibilities of international commerce very differently than I have seen it in my decades as an exporter. Let's take a careful look at some of their most common objections:

## A FLOOD OF CHEAP IMPORTS WILL DISPLACE AMERICAN-PRODUCED PRODUCTS

This is the easiest objection to allay. It is, in fact, baffling to me that we need to contend with it at all. Remember that our markets are already wide open to a vast majority of our trading partners. Most of the products exported to the United States by our top fifteen trading partners come in at near-zero tariffs. In 2008, our trade deficit with those fifteen countries was six hundred and thirty-three billion dollars—primarily because we do not have reciprocal low-tariff arrangements for our exports with many of these countries. The simple fact is that the flood of cheap imports has already happened—have you walked into a Walmart lately? That's why the argument against the aggressive pursuit of commerce with other nations seems so baffling to me.

The FTAs we have already negotiated but not enacted will not create less of a market for American-produced goods and American-based services. Rather, they will dramatically increase the market by giving American manufacturers and service providers greatly enhanced opportunities to sell their products all over the world. The same will be even truer of the Conscientious Equity Accords I am proposing. Using our pending FTA with Colombia as an example, such an agreement would remove barriers to U.S. service providers in key sectors such as construction, distribution, finance, information technologies, and telecommunications. It would finally give us access to these markets under the most favorable conditions, all in exchange for something that Colombia has already enjoyed for years.

## FTAs Trigger American Job Losses

Again, this notion is based on the assumption that American consumers will choose cheaper products created by foreign competitors, thereby stripping income from American businesses, which
will reduce work forces in response. As with the previous objection,
this logic is faulty, because, in most cases, those foreign products
are already on the shelves of American stores. FTAs have proven to
be an engine of job creation, not job reduction, and Conscientious
Equity Accords would build upon this further by improving conditions in foreign markets, boosting those countries' economies,
and allowing for larger sales of our products and services in those
markets. Simply go back to the numbers we discussed in the first
chapter of this book: three times as much business with Chile
since we signed our FTA with them, a fifty-five percent increase in
business with Australia, a thirty-five percent increase in business
with Singapore, and so on. These sales increases mean increases in
American jobs. Keep in mind that, dollar for dollar, our exports
employ nearly five times more people than our imports employ
and pay seventeen percent higher wages.

Agreements of this sort (especially if they are Conscientious
Equity Accords) have considerably greater value when one thinks
about building a larger trading platform with countries in our
hemisphere (which was the intention of the Colombian FTA that
Congress put on indefinite hold). In such a case, the only ones
who should be worried about losing jobs are the Chinese, who currently do a disproportionate share of business with our neighbors.
Logistic costs and transit times mean that offshore manufacturing in neighboring countries will make much more sense once we
have the necessary protections afforded by Conscientious Equity
Accords. Such considerations will move production of textiles and
other consumer goods closer to home. In addition, Latin American
producers are likely to use American-made raw materials such

as fiber, yarn, and fabrics in their production. This is why both the National Council of Textile Organizations and the National Cotton Council supported CAFTA (our free trade agreement with Central America and the Dominican Republic). A shirt that says, "Made in Colombia" is likely to contain more than fifty percent American content, whereas a shirt that says, "Made in China" probably has none.

## INTERNATIONAL TRADE LEAVES AMERICAN BUSINESSES UNPROTECTED

I have discussed many of the risks that American manufacturers and service providers face when dealing outside our borders, including corruption and theft of intellectual property. In fact, unless we chose to do *no* business with other countries (a course of action that would be disastrous to our economy and that not even the staunchest opponent of international commerce is suggesting), the only way to insure the protection of American businesses is through the kind of Conscientious Equity Accords I am suggesting here. We have already laid the groundwork for such accords. With each FTA we have negotiated, the protections inherent in the agreement have become stronger. The kind of comprehensive agreement that I advocate would make such protections even more ironclad. Considering the arcane nature of the dispute process in the WTO, accords negotiated with individual nations (or with nations within a particular region) offer us the only opportunity to guarantee that American businesses get fair treatment overseas.

For example, CAFTA (which passed in Congress by only one vote) strengthened intellectual property rights. It bases investment laws on core U.S. legal protections and due process. It includes some of the strongest language in this regard that we have ever had with a trading partner. These protections benefit not only

Americans, but Central Americans as well. The agreement includes a monitoring protocol for the enforcement of existing labor laws, as well as new transparency requirements that were not part of any previous FTA. These provisions will greatly help to promote and advance the rule of law that is at the heart of a functioning and peaceful society. If we had not ratified CAFTA, tens of thousands of Central Americans and Dominicans would have found their jobs moving to China. Poverty in these countries would have increased, with more illegal immigrants heading for our shores, providing another lose-lose scenario for the parties involved.

CAFTA has value beyond financial matters, as well. Important political and historical implications came along with this agreement. The emerging democracies on our southern border have aligned their futures with us. They have embraced democracy and our definition of fair commerce. CAFTA gave us the opportunity to reinforce these new democracies in our backyard. Think back just twenty years, when Castro-sponsored civil wars, Marxist Sandinistas, and leftist guerrillas ravished the region and were daily headlines in our media. Central America has rejected this situation and, bolstered by open trade with America, has no reason to turn back.

## AN EMPHASIS ON INTERNATIONAL COMMERCE ENCOURAGES DOING BUSINESS WITH CORRUPT GOVERNMENTS OR GOVERNMENTS THAT DON'T SHARE OUR VALUES

Sun Tzu, the author of *The Art of War*, advocated a simple philosophy more than twenty-five hundred years ago that rings as true now as it ever did: "Keep your friends close, and your enemies closer." One of the core missions of conscientious equity is to allow as many people as possible to benefit from better opportunities, fair treatment as human beings, improved labor standards, a cleaner environment, and a just legal system. Because of this mission, it is even more important that we boost the business we do with despotic governments—under the right, carefully negotiated circumstances—than the business we do with nations that already share our values. We have abundant evidence to show that we cannot force our way of life down the throats of nations and cultures that do not want it. Without the kind of formalized comprehensive agreements I envision with our Comprehensive Equity Accords, it is nearly impossible to spread our values in any way at all. Carefully and wisely presenting the terms under which we will continue to leave our market open to foreign goods and services and entering into accords that allow our entrepreneurs, the fruits of their labors, and our spirit to have a greater presence in nations whose governing philosophies we oppose will give us the basis to negotiate for the transparent laws, legal systems, human rights safeguards, and labor protections that will improve the lives of the people in those nations.

We currently do business with many countries that treat their people atrociously and deal with American entrepreneurs contemptuously. In the years I spent in Southeast Asia, I saw abundant examples of such behavior (I've already shared some examples, and there will be more in coming chapters). Continuing to do business with these governments without a formal accord that outlines a more enlightened way of dealing with their citizenry is tantamount to abetting a crime; in effect, we are endorsing criminal acts and criminal treatment. At the same time, walking away entirely would be even worse. As I mentioned in my discussion of trade sanctions, ending our trade relationship would prevent the people in these nations from witnessing and benefiting from the American example. There is only one acceptable answer, and our elected officials should be well informed enough to know it.

## FREE TRADE ENCOURAGES THE DESPOLIATION OF THE ENVIRONMENT

Again, the perspective of this argument is far too narrow. It suggests that our building a higher platform for international commerce will make the problem extreme—when it is *already* extreme and we are failing to use the only real leverage we have to help solve it.

Let's look at what China is doing and the impact of its actions on its neighbors. Though it has been a long time since the Chinese have been involved in any direct military engagement with the South Koreans, they have placed South Korea under vicious and constant attack by unleashing on it a deadly wave of airborne pollutants known as "yellow wind"—a lethal cocktail of dust, contaminants, and poisonous gases that target the immune system, causing respiratory disease, heart failure, and cancer. These massive dust storms that engulf the region are especially prevalent in the spring. For weeks each year, a toxic yellow haze covers Seoul. Officials cancel school and tell people to stay indoors because of a multitude of health risks. Acid rain pours down, poisoning lakes, rivers, forests, and crops. Numerous scientists believe that this phenomenon will accelerate and that it will have an impact on the western United States within a decade. Others suggest that you can already detect the effects of yellow wind as far away from China as Kansas.

The dust mixes with billions of tons of carbon dioxide and other pollutants that China emits each year into the atmosphere. Most of China's emissions come from its coal-fired electrical generation plants and furnaces. China brings online an average of one coal-fired power plant every week. It is its stated policy to do so for years to come. These plants are quick and inexpensive to build using technology developed just after World War II. They have a lifespan of seventy-five years, meaning that they will be spewing out death and destruction for decades to come. China already burns more coal than the United States, the EU, and Japan combined. The Chinese justify their coal consumption by pointing out that the United States and Europe committed their own environmental atrocities during the Industrial Revolution. Since the Chinese are going through the equivalent of this revolution now, they claim that they must be allowed a certain amount of leeway with regard to environmental standards as they power up. The Chinese are not wrong in calling the West out for its abuses of the environment in decades past. There is one enormous difference though: back then, we were largely unaware of what we were doing to the planet. The Chinese, however, know exactly what is going on, because the data are readily available to them. The Chinese also have a choice to invest in cleaner technologies, including clean-coal technology, but they don't seem to want to take the time or spend the money.

The deforestation of China's north and northwest provinces has created a large desert wasteland. Decades of timber exploitation, slash-and-burn farming techniques, and population growth have resulted in desiccation and the elimination of water resources as plant life disappears, rainfall shrinks, and lakes disappear. More than fifty percent of China's land is either arid or semi-arid, mostly as a result of human activities. As China has destroyed forever much of its forests, it has turned to the ecologically sensitive tropical rainforests of Kalimantan (the Indonesian portion of Borneo), where corrupt officials are plentiful and ready to plunder natural resources for a price. After the Indonesians clear these forests of their valuable timber to sell to the Chinese, they set them on fire to make way for sprawling agricultural estates. These fires often burn out of control for weeks until the monsoon rains arrive. A highly toxic, thick black cloud covers the region, poisoning more than one hundred and fifty million of the people living in Indonesia, Singapore, Malaysia, Brunei, the Philippines, and southern Thailand. Pygmy elephants, clouded leopards, gibbons, orangutans, sun bears, and rhinoceroses are just a few of the species hovering on the edge of extinction in these polluted regions.

It would be irresponsible to believe that the wanton destruction of China's environment and the surrounding region is China's problem alone. An American trade policy that allows China free access to our market without conditions is a chief contributor to the greatest environmental meltdown in the history of our planet. More than thirty percent of Chinese emissions are the direct result of exports for consumption by the United States and the EU. The destruction of Southeast Asia's tropical rainforests is rife with our fingerprints. We have been willing participants in these horrific crimes.

Of course, it is unfair to target China alone. The clear-cutting of the Amazonian rainforest for the purpose of harvesting lumber and creating more grazing land is an environmental apocalypse. We are losing tens of thousands of plant and animal species every year for the sake of cheap wood and fast food. More than half of the Amazonian rainforest—an irreplaceable resource for everything from food to shelter to medicine—has been eviscerated in a little more than half a century. Because many consider this rainforest the "lungs of the world," we could be said to be performing a protracted and painful form of suicide. Again, we are very much to blame because our conspicuous consumption drives much of this deforestation.

This is the world that exists right now—a world that we can help remedy by changing the way we do business with China, Brazil, and any other nation that despoils its environment and puts us all at grave risk. The only possible solution to these environmental travesties is a bilateral Conscientious Equity Accord that includes strict environmental language and the necessary safeguards to ensure that this language becomes law in the offending nations. Sticking to the status quo is not only unacceptable; it is also unsustainable.

Lest I be guilty of the same chauvinism toward the U.S. environmental policy that other countries practice, it is hard to ignore the U.S. government's inept approach to cleaning up the 2010 BP oil spill in the Gulf of Mexico. While tens of millions of gallons of oil spewed into once pristine habitats, wiping out aquatic life and the livelihoods of thousands of residents who relied on the Gulf for income, the Obama administration stood on the sidelines and let BP, who caused the spill, take control of cleanup operations. It might take decades for this area to recover from this, the worst environmental disaster in U.S. history.

The ultimate blame for this environmental catastrophe rests not only with BP, but with a deeply flawed energy policy that allowed for deep-water drilling without proper oversight and a contingency plan in the event of an oil spill of this magnitude. A tenet of Conscientious Equity is never to allow greed to blind a country's eye toward proper environmental stewardship. Let us hope that as the United States explores new energy options we are never again responsible for visiting such devastation on the world's delicate ecosystem.

## RAISING THE BAR OR RAISING THE ROOF

I would also guess that at this point in this book, you understand how the objections that stand as barriers to our pending FTAs and the more comprehensive Conscientious Equity Accords that I am advocating hold little water. The question, then, is this: if you understand, why do so few of our politicians?

Of course, some of politicians' reluctance to embrace trade agreements is purely about constituencies. The labor vote is tremendously important for politicians in many parts of the country. It is disproportionately important in the swing states that have a profound impact on national elections, and the AFL-CIO is staunchly opposed to "free trade." On May 21, 2009, Thea Lea, policy director of the AFL-CIO, testified before the Senate Finance Committee regarding our pending FTA with Panama. She took this opportunity to present her organization's general position on our trade policies:

Current US trade policy has failed to deliver good jobs at home; equitable, democratic, and sustainable development abroad; or a

stable global economy. We need to review and reform our trade
policy with respect to the overall framework of rules; our chronic
and large trade imbalances; and the impact of our trade and investment policies on US manufacturers, farmers, service providers,
consumers, workers, and the environment. Nor should trade policy impinge on the ability of democratically elected governments
at the federal, state, or local level to implement and enforce public
policies designed to achieve legitimate social objectives.

This review is especially urgent in light of the current economic
crisis, and the weakness of the US labor market. As long as we
continue to run trade deficits on the order of five percent of GDP,
the arguments that we need more trade liberalization to succeed in
the global economy ring hollow—especially to our members, who
have seen too many jobs go offshore while their wages and benefits
stagnate.

US competitiveness should not be assessed based on the prof-
itability of US multinational corporations operating abroad, but
rather on the ability of US-based producers to compete and thrive
on American soil in a dynamic global economy. By this standard,
our trade policy needs deep reform. Consideration of new trade
agreements should happen only in the context of broad trade policy reform.[6]

Essentially, Lea is saying that we need to cease any efforts to move
forward until we have a new plan fully in place. The AFL-CIO
has a history of forestalling giving its support as a way of pas-
sive-aggressively avoiding giving support altogether. "Broad trade
policy reform"—frankly, the kind of reform I advocate in this
book—takes years to implement and requires negotiation on an
international level. If the AFL-CIO withholds its support, essentially telling its membership to vote only for candidates that advocate against building international commerce, our elected officials
will continue to shy away from tackling this issue. Therefore, the
unions have set up the perfect Catch-22 for their purposes: they

won't endorse our trade policy without an overhaul, and the politicians that usually receive the labor vote won't pursue the policy changes that would lead to an overhaul without AFL-CIO endorsement.

Unions oppose trade agreements for all the wrong reasons. The unions are against the agreements because union members represent a small portion of our workforce (though they are a large portion in certain swing states) and have legacy deals that are uncompetitive in the world economy and cannot be justified. International commerce threatens the inequity of these deals and drives employers to contend with the folly of dealing with an over-salaried organization. Simply look at the GM workers who were paid very well to stay home, and compare their wages to "right-to-work state" wages. GM was paying its employees thirty-eight percent more in Detroit than Toyota was paying its non-union employees in Tennessee. Is it any wonder that the AFL-CIO won't allow most foreign cars in its parking lots?

The most ironic thing about this is that union workers themselves—who vote against candidates who support a vigorous trade policy because their union leaders tell them to do so—would benefit significantly from increasing the business we do overseas. They have already lost the jobs they are so concerned about losing, because we are a duty-free market. Our trade agreements always lead to more business overall and always tip the balance of trade in our favor. The Conscientious Equity Accords I discuss in this book would accomplish these outcomes even more dramatically because they would improve the economies of our trading partners, thereby, creating a more hospitable environment for our products. That would mean more American manufacturing, and more work for those in the manufacturing sector.

So what do we do to force the issue with our politicians? How do we let them know that their ill-informed positions are out of touch with our most pressing needs? We need to start treating our politicians like entrepreneurs. All good entrepreneurs know that they must keep their ears to the ground, anticipate shifts in the market, and react accordingly. When threatened with extinction, entrepreneurs make the changes necessary to survive. We need to send a message to our politicians—through letters, through the media, and, most important, through the ballot box—that a shift is underway. We must to let them know that we no longer accept their undereducated responses to an issue as vital to our future as international commerce. We must demand that they pay attention to the facts and stop pandering to organizations that speak only for a small minority (for example, the AFL-CIO has approximately thirteen million members, equal to less than six percent of the adult population of the United States, yet its influence is exponentially greater because of where its membership is concentrated).

If I have made my points at all persuasively at this stage, then you know that the ignorance and limited view of many of our elected officials is completely unacceptable. If you believe in Conscientious Equity, then no one who doesn't believe in it deserves your vote.

## CHAPTER NINE

# OUR MOST VALUABLE IMPORTS

THE CONCEPT OF CONSCIENTIOUS EQUITY stands for many things. Certainly, it is about creating global commerce in new and enlightened ways. It is also about using American purchasing power to drive reforms on which good people from all over the world agree. In addition, it is about creating a shining example, one that is inclusive and that embraces all the good people of the world.

As I have previously stated, I present this book from an American perspective. From that perspective, I see a kind of confusion on the issue of immigration—the ultimate expression of inclusiveness—that is at odds with the precepts of Conscientious Equity.

For many years, a debate has been raging about whether or not we should toughen our immigration laws and close our doors to those who seek to leave their ancestral homes to settle in America. From the standpoint of the highest aims of Conscientious Equity, setting up barriers to immigration seems terribly wrong. Conscientious Equity is about giving everyone a stake in the future, and denying anyone who uses the proper channels (more on this in a bit) to seek a life within our borders that future would conflict with that goal. Let's look at this from a more practical standpoint, as well: immigrants are tremendously good for our economy.

You may be surprised to learn that the very foundation of the Internet rests on the brilliant minds of immigrants who came to America for the opportunity to live the American dream. One of the founders of Google is Sergey Brin, who was born in Moscow, Russia. Institutional anti-Semitism drove Brin's highly educated parents to exit their homeland. Sergey, his parents, and his father's mother, were granted exit visas to leave the former Soviet Union in May 1979. Five months later, they arrived in New York and, shortly thereafter, settled in Maryland. Sergey received his under-graduate degree from the University of Maryland in mathematics and computer science. A National Science Foundation scholarship allowed him to pursue graduate studies at Stanford University, where he met fellow graduate student Larry Page. In January 1996, the two friends started a research project that eventually became Google, Inc.

Google has embraced immigrants into its workforce. For example, Omid Kordestani, who was born in Iran, moved to California as a teenager, and became a senior vice president of Google. Addressing the 2007 graduating class at San Jose State University, he said, "To keep my edge, I must think and act like an immigrant. There is a special optimism and drive that I have benefited from and continue to rely on that I want all of you to find. . . . Immigrants are inherently dreamers and fighters."[1]

Two of the three people who launched YouTube were also immigrants: Steven Chen, originally from Taiwan, and Jawed Karim, born in Germany. Immigrants also helped start Yahoo!, eBay, and Sun Microsystems.

What could be more American than steel? Yet most people have forgotten that the U.S. steel industry was largely built by Andrew Carnegie, whose family emigrated from Scotland in the 1800s. In 1889, the steel output of the United States was more than that of the United Kingdom and the majority of American steel came from the Carnegie Steel plant.

The next time you gaze at the East Wing of the National Gallery of Art in Washington, D.C.; the John F. Kennedy Memorial Library in Boston; or the Rock and Roll Hall of Fame in Cleveland, thank architect I. M. Pei, whose family emigrated to the United States from the Guangdong province in southern China. When you enjoy a Pepsi or Coke, keep in mind that Indra Nooyi, who went to college in the southern Indian city of Chennai and earned an MBA in Kolkata, is the CEO of PepsiCo and that Roberto C. Goizueta, a Cuban exile, led Coca-Cola through most of the eighties and nineties. Ralph de la Vega, who was a "Pedro Pan" baby born in Cuba and sent to America as a young boy without his parents after the upheaval of the Cuban Revolution, is today the president of AT&T Mobility.

If we choose to stop attracting visionaries like these to the United States, we will become less competitive in the world. Immigration is a tremendously powerful force—a force that helps our country compete in an increasingly competitive world.

## TOWARD A SANE IMMIGRATION POLICY

The Woodrow Wilson International Center for Scholars 2006 Migration Policy Institute Report notes:

No country can afford to have an immigration system that either ignores or otherwise merely ratifies the facts on the ground. Yet, that is what the United States has been doing for a while now. The result is a challenge to the most basic rules of governance; a hit-or-miss relationship between immigration policy and crucial US economic and social priorities; and an exceptional degree of political attention, not all of which has been thoughtful or productive.[2]

In this same vein, the Center for an Urban Future, a nonprofit study group in New York, found that highly successful immigrants are having a big impact on the economies of American cities:

> During the past decade, immigrants have been the entrepreneurial sparkplugs of cities from New York to Los Angeles—starting a greater share of new businesses than native-born residents, stimulating growth in sectors from food manufacturing to health care, creating loads of new jobs, and transforming once-sleepy neighborhoods into thriving commercial centers. And immigrant entrepreneurs are also becoming one of the most dependable parts of cities' economies: while elite sectors like finance (New York), entertainment (Los Angeles) and energy (Houston) fluctuate wildly through cycles of boom and bust, immigrants have been starting businesses and creating jobs during both good times and bad.[3]

These attitudes really put immigration in perspective, especially as America grapples with the estimated twelve million *undocumented* workers currently in this country. The word "undocumented" has become a lighting rod for groups rallying against immigration. Among these undocumented workers, however, are people with real skills that can contribute to our economy. In fact, writing for the Newspaper Enterprise Association, Cokie Roberts and Steven V. Roberts wrote:

> The debate focuses mainly on the twelve million undocumented workers in America, but another group is equally important: the

highly educated immigrants who want to live and work in this country, but are driven away by its stupid and self-defeating policies.

Every economist agrees: Skilled immigrants are job-creating engines.

Moreover, ideas have no boundaries. The United States will not prosper by making cheaper goods than Bangladesh; it will only grow richer by remaining a mecca for innovation and imagination. We're locked in a worldwide competition for the best and the brightest minds, and we're falling behind.[4]

The Robertses continued with a quote from an article in the Canadian magazine *Maclean's* entitled "Stealing Talent from Uncle Sam," which details how Canadian officials are recruiting professionals in California. They are successful, according to the publication, because of America's outdated and complicated visa process. "The longer Uncle Sam takes to get his house in order, the better it is for us," the article suggested.

## FIXING A FLAWED VISA POLICY

When it comes to the status of immigrant workers, most Americans are familiar with employment-based green cards, which permit permanent residency. However, there is more to the immigrant story. Citizens of most foreign countries require a visa to enter the United States. Visas issued at U.S. consulates and embassies abroad allow an individual to travel to a U.S. port of entry and request permission to enter the country. There are two main types of U.S. visas: immigrant visas and non-immigrant visas. Immigrant visas are for individuals who intend to live permanently in the United States. Non-immigrant visas are for individuals with permanent residence outside of the United States who wish to be in the country on a temporary basis.

There is another visa, however. As of this writing, the H-1B visa has created a political firestorm, because U.S. businesses have put pressure on Congress to remove the barriers that tend to drag out a process that would allow swift entry to the United States for the very type of highly skilled worker we need to remain competitive. The skills needed to stay competitive are often not available at home. Our schools and universities are simply not turning out the engineers, mathematicians, scientists, doctors, and other professionals needed to sustain the economy of a superpower. Notwithstanding, getting our educational infrastructure aligned with the global economy will take time; we will always need the skills of immigrants to build our country. Taking this into consideration, the H-1B visa also allows companies to hire foreign-born graduates of American universities. These visas are usually reserved for immigrants with special skills operating in "specialty occupations," especially in the high-tech area.

The regulations define a "specialty occupation" as requiring theoretical and practical application of a body of highly specialized knowledge in a field of human endeavor, such as, but not limited to, architecture, engineering, mathematics, physical sciences, social sciences, biotechnology, medicine and health, education, law, accounting, business specialties, theology, or the arts. Applicants are required to have attained a bachelor's degree or its equivalent as a minimum.

In May of 2010, nearly ninety members of the U.S. House of Representatives co-sponsored an immigration reform bill that would make broad changes to the H-1B visa program. The proposed legislation is designed to create a new, independent federal agency, to be called the Commission on Immigration and Labor Markets, that would establish "employment-based immigration policies that promote economic growth and competitiveness while minimizing job displacement, wage depression and unauthorized employment." In particular, the new agency would make recommendations to Congress about caps for H-1Bs and other types of visas.[5]

There's another visa option that was discussed in some detail during the George W. Bush administration. The Guest Worker Visa Program was intended as a way to allow U.S. employers to sponsor non-U.S. citizens as laborers for approximately three years. This has great merit because it allows employers to "cherry pick" those foreign workers who could do the most good for their individual businesses. The drawback to the proposed program is that it doesn't have enough controls in place to monitor the length of a foreign worker's stay. If such a worker elects to leave the job he or she was hired for before the three-year period ends, that person essentially becomes an undocumented worker. At the very least, we would need to conduct extensive background checks to eliminate applicants guilty of crimes either in the United States or abroad.

Some new thinking about the Guest Worker visa program would actually help the economy. Instead of draining U.S. resources, immigrants would be required to pay all taxes related to their employment. This is a program with a real upside and one that the federal government should explore more deeply.

New approaches of this sort will help keep other countries from poaching the best and the brightest who want to seek new opportunities in America.

## A DELICATE BALANCING ACT

One of the inequities built into our current immigration policy is that we must differentiate between immigrants who come to this country legally to establish roots and contribute to our economy and those who come to this country illegally, especially those who may harbor feelings of ill will toward our way of life. We are a nation of laws that must be respected. That means we are obligated to secure our borders to ensure the safety of our nation and, and we must demand that everyone play by the rules. We must not reward bad behavior by granting amnesty to illegal immigrants who choose not to go through legal immigration status. Our borders must be secured and we must be willing to devote the resources required to stop the flow of illegal immigrants.

I know firsthand how difficult it can be to go through the proper channels to legally immigrate. Although I am a U.S. citizen, when I was living in Manila I had to stand in long lines for hours and wait six months before my wife of twelve years completed the immigration process and could legally immigrate to the United States. Yes, it was frustrating and lengthy, but when you think about the value of the prize at the end of the process—U.S. citizenship—it was worth the hardship.

Literally millions of people around the globe respect our laws and are waiting their turn for a piece of the American dream. They must not be demeaned by equating them with the millions who trample on our laws through illegal immigration. We cannot reward immigrants who seek a shortcut to living in this country by thumbing their noses at the very system of laws that will protect them if they follow the legal path to citizenship.

Through my many years of work in exporting American products and promoting entrepreneurship, I have often been in contact with students from Africa, Asia, Europe, the Middle East, and Latin America who are getting their degrees at American universities and staying on to work for American manufacturers and exporters. I have worked with immigrants from every corner of the world who have established trading companies to sell American products in every market imaginable. Immigrants often become our greatest promoters and our window to the world. They have made enormous contributions to America's export industry and to our country.

## STOPPING THE BRAIN DRAIN

We should never forget that immigrants founded this country. They came to America seeking an opportunity to make a new life in a country with unlimited prospects and freedoms. Most stayed here, but others chose to gain an education and leave. In other cases, restrictions were put in the way of talented men and women who wanted to live in America but were denied access. Both scenarios have led to a "brain drain." The brains and talents that can keep our country in the forefront of technology, research and development, business startups, and medicine are taking their expertise elsewhere because we are making things too hard for them. This simply must stop.

America needs to hang out its "Open for Business" sign and welcome talented immigrants to our country. We cannot become the nation of exclusivity when our very founding was based on inclusiveness. Let us never forget, "Give me your tired, your poor, your huddled masses yearning to breathe free, The wretched refuse of your teeming shore. Send these, the homeless, tempest-tossed to me, I lift my lamp beside the golden door!"

We must prove that these words continue to ring true today. Let us agree to establish a sound immigration policy that affords opportunities for success in this country to those who abide by the rules and are committed to the ideal of the American dream.

This willingness to do what is right for those who want to contribute to America's preeminence as the land of opportunity is as important as any part of Conscientious Equity. The immigrant success story in America ultimately lifts up and brings light to millions of citizens everywhere. This is an achievement of which we can all be proud.

## CHAPTER TEN

# THAT'S WHY THEY CALL HIM "CHIEF EXECUTIVE"

CORDELL HULL WAS A MAN OF MANY ACCOMPLISHMENTS. He was a Nobel Prize winner. He was the longest-serving secretary of state in American history. He was a congressman for eleven terms, a senator for part of one term (interrupted by his appointment as secretary of state), and a chair of the Democratic National Committee. Most people remember him for his role as one of the primary initiators of the United Nations, for which he won the Nobel Prize. Before he set to that task, however, he engineered a bit of consensus building that had a profound impact on the way we do business around the world.

The year was 1934, the world was deep in economic depression, the Smoot-Hawley Act had driven American tariffs through the roof, and countries around the world were taking increasingly aggressive protectionist measures. From Hull's perspective, lowering trade barriers was a key part of turning around the financial fortunes of America and the world. However, Congress, whose members were dependent on myriad special interests and regional needs, would have trouble dropping these barriers.

Unfortunately for Hull, Congress held all the cards. Section 8 of Article 1 of the U.S. Constitution clearly gives Congress the right to "regulate commerce with foreign nations" and "to lay and collect taxes, duties, imposts, and excises." Somehow, Hull, through a particularly inspired bit of diplomacy that presaged his Nobel-Prize-winning efforts, persuaded Congress to grant the president the power to make foreign trade agreements. The Reciprocal Trade Agreements Act (RTAA) turned congressional power over to the president in a limited way, allowing him specifically to enter into pacts in which America would lower its tariffs in exchange for a reciprocal decrease in tariffs by a foreign nation. This was a huge step toward building business with foreign countries after the days of Smoot-Hawley (and an extremely rare instance of the legislative branch voluntarily ceding power to the executive branch).[1]

Congress did not let go of power easily. Legislators debated the act for four months before voting on it. They took an extremely active role in developing a limited list of terms—and only those terms—that the State Department could grant in new trade agreements. They insisted on our having a "most-favored nation" position in any agreement, which would require any foreign government to offer trade policies to the United States better than those offered to any other nation. They demanded that any reductions in tariffs happen on a product-specific basis (as opposed to lowering tariffs with a particular country on all items). They set strict guidelines regarding acceptable levels of reductions of this sort and required that such reductions happen only after "exhaustive study shows that they will not result in material injury to any group of American producers."[2] Most significant, they granted this license to the president for a limited term, requiring him to petition Congress for renewal on a biannual basis.

Still, the RTAA made trade negotiations overwhelmingly easier than they had been before. In the thirteen years between 1934 and 1947 (when GATT took effect), the president made trade agreements with twenty-nine countries and reduced tariffs by a total of nearly fifty percent.[3]

The president continued to have the power granted by the RTAA until 1962, when the Trade Expansion Act of 1962, with a specific eye toward negotiating agreements with the European Common Market, gave President Kennedy wider powers. Through this act, Kennedy created the Office of the Special Trade Representative and appointed two deputies—one in Washington and one in Geneva—to make policy recommendations. This act led to tariff reductions for American goods throughout Europe.

## MOVING ONTO THE FAST TRACK—AND FALLING OFF

The Trade Act of 1974 took matters even further, granting the president "fast track" authority to pursue trade agreements around the world that Congress could approve or disapprove but could not amend or filibuster. This authority, known as Trade Promotion Authority (TPA), gave the president true trade negotiation power for the first time, finally putting him on equal footing with heads of state from developed nations all around the world.

Every president from 1974 to 1994 had TPA, though each had to petition Congress for the right to hold onto it. In 1995, and again in 1997, Congress denied President Clinton's petition. The denial hinged on the president's treatment of labor and the environment in his petition, but it also had something to do with the shift in party power after the 1994 midterm elections. TPA remained lapsed until 2002 when, in one of the most hotly contested and partisan pieces of trade legislation ever, Congress agreed *by one vote* to give it to President Bush. As you have seen in this book, the president used this authority to negotiate several significant, if not sizeable, FTAs. These agreements went before Congress and passed—until the Colombian vote languished. On June 30, 2007, the president's TPA expired. To date, there has been little conversation in either house about renewing it, even now that a new president has taken office and his party controls both the House of Representatives and the Senate.

The problems with rescinding TPA are manifold. Chief among them is how it weakens America's position at the negotiating table with other heads of state. In an op-ed piece in the *Wall Street Journal*, C. Fred Bergsten, of the Peterson Institute for International Economics, writes, "Without arrangements that assure reasonably prompt congressional action on agreements negotiated by the president, other countries legitimately fear that Congress will simply let deals languish, or insist on further concessions."[4] He further notes that, under such circumstances, other countries "will not engage seriously with the United States in either multilateral or bilateral talks."

We have already seen the impact of conducting trade negotiations without TPA. The refusal by Congress to vote on Colombia and Panama (and on the FTA we negotiated with Korea, which has much bigger trade implications) has put those agreements in extended—and perhaps even permanent—limbo. President Obama, who has stated that he plans to reopen these negotiations, cannot do so with any hope of success as long as the leaders of that country (like those of Colombia and Korea) believe that the subsequent agreements will be subject to endless amendment by Congress.

The president will face similar reticence from any new nation that he seeks to engage in trade talks. This puts us in an untenable position at a time when China, the EU, and even Mexico are aggressively signing FTAs and we lack such agreements with most of our largest trading partners. "It sends a negative signal to the rest of the world that we're confused on trade policy and temporarily bowing out of negotiations," remarked Daniel T. Griswold, director of the Center for Trade Policy Studies at the CATO Institute in 2007, when it appeared clear that Congress was not going to renew TPA.[5]

This has been true when the president has been trying to negotiate only free trade agreements. How much more difficult will it be to have our chief executive attempting to sit down with our partners to hammer out comprehensive Conscientious Equity Accords if those partners aren't convinced that he has the will of Congress to do so? Conscientious Equity Accords are about much more than reduced tariffs. They are about addressing and rectifying significant worldwide social issues. They are about job creation here and abroad. They are about raising the American tax *base* so we can stop talking about raising the American tax *rate*. Generating these accords will require lengthy and carefully orchestrated negotiations. The last thing with which our president needs to be concerned during these negotiations is whether Congress is going to make him do back flips once he comes to an agreement.

TPA does something else: it tells the president that growing international commerce is a very important part of his agenda. TPA isn't a perk of the office, like a four-year membership at Camp David. It is a mandate to the person in that office to generate more business for America overseas. In a Conscientious Equity world, it is a further mandate to use this business to do good work for all people. If we believe that Conscientious Equity Accords raise everyone, then we need to give our president the power to achieve such accords—and the clear message that it is his duty to do so.

## THE ARGUMENT AGAINST TRADE PROMOTION AUTHORITY

Those who argue against TPA fall into one of two camps. Some oppose TPA simply because the Constitution says that this authority belongs to another branch of government. To me, the answer to this argument is the same as the one that stops people from complaining about getting older: consider the alternative. The alternative in this case is leaving responsibility for trade promotion in the hands of Congress. This kind of thinking led to Smoot-Hawley and the roller-coaster trade policies that I have catalogued elsewhere in this book. Special interests have an even bigger voice in Washington than they did before the Reciprocal Trade Agreements Act in 1934. It is not difficult to imagine the kind of impact those special interests could have on negotiations with our biggest trading partners. In fact, it was precisely the avoidance of this kind of endless debate that drove Cordell Hull to seek the act—and Congress to pass it—in the first place.

The other major argument against TPA relates to the fear that such authority allows the president to run around making agreements unchecked by the legislative branch, whose only power would be to accept or reject the deal. An examination of the conditions under which the president received this authority in 2002 shows how specious this argument is. Before President Bush could enter into trade negotiations with any other country, he needed to give Congress ninety days notice. He then needed to consult with Congress and all congressional committees and oversight groups throughout his negotiations, and, according to an issue brief on this subject prepared for the One Hundred Seventh Congress, "Congress could withdraw expedited procedures if consultation requirements were not met."[6] Beyond this, the latest version of TPA gave the president a laundry list of provisions that he had to negotiate into any free trade agreement. These included intellectual property protection, safeguards against corruption, labor rights protection, and a suite of guidelines regarding rules of law.

Therefore, although it was the president and his designees sitting at the negotiating table, the voice of Congress was whispering in their ears the entire time. The legislative branch was, therefore, still very much involved in the process, and no one is suggesting we change this. Congress had a strong voice in the FTAs that President Bush negotiated and will continue to have a strong voice in any negotiations conducted by any other president to whom it grants TPA.

## MAKING A PERMANENT CHANGE FOR THE BETTER

What Congress should not have is the right to hold the president hostage every two years with regard to TPA. It makes us seem remarkably weak as a nation to have the head of our government go hat in hand to request the right to wield a power that virtually every other leader in the developed world already has. Anyone who has ever negotiated anything knows that one's opponent will only take one's demands seriously if he knows that one has the power to make such demands. If foreign governments believe that our president's power might disappear in the middle of negotiations, this puts us in an extremely poor negotiating position.

The executive branch is the only place where we can accomplish all that we must do to move our international commerce policies toward Conscientious Equity effectively and efficiently. I believe, therefore, that it is essential that we grant the president *permanent* authority in this arena. The Bretton Woods Committee, a "bipartisan, non-profit group organized to build public under-standing of international financial and development issues" which includes among its members President Carter, President George H. W. Bush, and former secretaries of state for both parties, states, "The absence of permanent trade promotion authority has under-mined successive administrations' efforts to liberalize trade and promote growth in the United States and global economy. This is ultimately costly for American jobs and profits, and damaging to our nation's international reputation."[7]

We can grant the president permanent TPA through a con-stitutional amendment, but such an amendment would require extraordinary levels of consensus and could take decades to accomplish. Much easier to achieve is an act of Congress. In fact, it is no harder procedurally to grant the president this kind of permanent authority than it is to grant him such authority for two years (though, admittedly, the level of debate might be consider-ably more strenuous).

I am not the first person to suggest this policy. In fact, there was an effort to grant the president permanent TPA in 2001, but it failed under the weight of special interests and partisanship. If anyone in Congress appreciated irony, he or she would have found plenty in a movement dying for the precise reason that the move-ment was necessary.

My guess is that any attempt to make TPA permanent would suffer a similar fate now. What is required to move Congress to action is that it embrace the paradigm shift I present in this book. I don't want the president to have *Trade Promotion* Authority; I want him to have *Conscientious Equity* Authority. The differences are profound. As I noted earlier, the term "free trade" carries far too much baggage. It suggests to many the fears of floods of cheap imports in our stores and the hemorrhaging of jobs that we have discussed (and allayed) elsewhere in these pages. More to the point, although generating more business for our exporters is nice, trade is the beginning of the conversation we need to have with other nations, not the object of that conversation. The far bigger objective is convincing countries around the world to band behind a set of ideals that should be a priority for all good people—including the good people in our own Congress. By putting the argument for permanent Conscientious Equity Authority in this context, I think it is unassailable.

CHAPTER ELEVEN

# CREATING A NEW ORGANIZATION

THE U.S. TRADE REPRESENTATIVE (USTR) recommends trade policy to the president and sits at the negotiating table with governments around the world to establish bilateral trade agreements, navigate through disputes, and establish other forms of trade policy.[1] As I'm sure is clear to you by now, international commerce is vitally important to the economic health of America and to the safety, security, and welfare of not only Americans but all citizens of the world. Therefore, one would assume that the USTR would serve a powerful role in the government, that this person would have extensive experience as both a negotiator and an exporter, and that any number of people would be desperate to have this role.

As it turns out, this is not particularly true. As I write this, the USTR in the Obama administration is Ron Kirk. Ron Kirk was a popular mayor of Dallas and a successful lawyer, but he has no obvious prior trade experience. It is entirely possible that, by the time this book comes off the presses, we will have a new USTR. After all, there were three during the George W. Bush administration. Robert Zoellick served from 2001 to 2005 before becoming deputy secretary of state. Rob Portman served from 2005 to 2006 before becoming director of the Office of Management and Budget. Susan Schwab then became USTR for the remainder of the Bush presidency. Portman and Schwab at least had trade experience before they took their turns in the role.

## A DIFFERENT MEANING FOR THE WORD "GLOBAL"

The USTR is a cabinet-level position. According to the Web site of the Office of the United States Trade Representative, the USTR "coordinates trade policy, resolves disagreements, and frames issues for presidential decision." The site continues, the "USTR consults with other government agencies on trade policy matters through the Trade Policy Review Group and the Trade Policy Staff Committee. More than a dozen government agencies, commissions, and international courts have jurisdiction over some aspect of international trade. Many of these agencies work closely with USTR; others operate in a separate arena."[2] My guess is that this level of consultation might be a primary reason why the office of the USTR has had a revolving door in recent administrations.

Here, very briefly, is a rundown of the agencies that have some role in managing our trade policy:

### DEPARTMENT OF COMMERCE

The International Trade Administration, a division of the Commerce Department, focuses on trade policy. Within this umbrella organization, several individual organizations contribute to the trade promotion and trade enforcement effort: The Import Administration serves as a watchdog for U.S. companies against the unfair trade practices of foreign organizations. The Trade Information Center acts as a research resource. The Trade Development unit offers help to small businesses and draws up (according to the USTR Web site, which is the source for all of the quoted passages in this section of the chapter) "retaliation lists that maximize penalties to offending trade partners and minimize their impact on the United States." The U.S. Commercial Service acts as a chamber of commerce to promote U.S. exports. Finally, the BuyUSA program matches U.S. products and services with international companies.

Other divisions of the Commerce Department are also involved with trade policy. The Bureau of the Census maintains foreign trade statistics. The U.S. Bureau of Industry and Security "regulates export of sensitive goods and technologies, and cooperates with other countries on export control and strategic trade issues." The Patent and Trademark Office helps protect American intellectual property outside our borders.

## DEPARTMENT OF LABOR

The Department of Labor's Bureau of International Affairs acts as a liaison with other government agencies regarding international trade and labor policies. It also polices the child labor standards in our FTAs and monitors the effect of our trade and immigration policies on American workers.

## DEPARTMENT OF HEALTH AND HUMAN SERVICES

Three organizations within the Department of Health and Human Services have input on trade policy. The Food and Drug Administration (FDA) serves as a consumer watchdog regarding the safety of our imports and exports. The Office of Regulatory

Affairs has an import program that oversees import regulations and alerts the American public about imports that have been barred from the country for health reasons. The Office of International Affairs operates in concert with the FDA to regulate the entry of foreign products into the United States and to negotiate entry of American products into foreign markets.

## DEPARTMENT OF AGRICULTURE

The Foreign Agriculture Service is the Department of Agriculture's primary conduit to market development overseas. The Foreign Agriculture Service plays an active role in negotiating trade agreements and plays multiple financial roles, from guaranteeing credit to providing food aid and helping increase income and food availability, in developing countries.

## DEPARTMENT OF THE TREASURY

Under the Department of the Treasury, the U.S. Customs Service enforces tariffs and works to keep illegal goods out of the United States. Meanwhile, the Office of Foreign Assets Control (OFAC) "administers and enforces economic and trade sanctions against targeted foreign countries, terrorism-sponsoring organizations and international narcotics traffickers based on U.S. foreign policy and national security goals." OFAC has the authority to freeze foreign assets if the president deems this necessary.

## DEPARTMENT OF JUSTICE

The Department of Justice's Computer Crime and Intellectual Property Section acts as the American agency involved in the international effort to fight computer crime. It also enforces the Economic Espionage Act, which metes out punishment for the theft of trade secrets.

## DEPARTMENT OF TRANSPORTATION

More than ninety-five percent of our imports and exports travel on a ship at some point in the delivery process. The Coast Guard therefore has a role in our trade process, as it is actively involved in setting the rules that apply to the shipping industry throughout the world. The Coast Guard also works in concert with the U.S. Customs Service to prevent illegal goods from gaining entry to our country. Meanwhile, the Federal Highway Administration influences international trade as it relates to the trucking of Canadian and Mexican goods on American roads.

## DEPARTMENT OF STATE

Within the Department of State, the Bureau of Economic and Business Affairs promotes U.S. business interests overseas. The Bureau's Trade Policy and Programs Division advances economic prosperity by increasing trade through the opening of overseas markets and freeing the flow of goods, services, and capital. The division works closely with USTR and other government agencies to expand open market approaches to trade; enforce rules and agreements to reduce and eliminate foreign trade barriers, increase transparency, and strengthen the rule of law; combat foreign competitive practices that impede U.S. access to markets; and promote U.S. trade interests within the WTO and regional trade organizations such as the Asia-Pacific Economic Cooperation (APEC), the NAFTA Secretaria, and the Free Trade Area of the Americas.

## FEDERAL TRADE COMMISSION

The Federal Trade Commission (FTC) monitors the actions of foreign companies in an attempt to thwart market distortions. The

FTC "seeks to ensure that the nation's markets function competitively, and are vigorous, efficient, and free of undue restrictions."

## ENVIRONMENTAL PROTECTION AGENCY

The Environmental Protection Agency's Office of International
Affairs works with governments around the world to set international environmental policy and establish standards for environmental quality. The Office of Pesticides Programs monitors our
international pacts to ensure that our agreements regarding the use
of chemicals are consistent with the standards we have set at home.

## U.S. TRADE AND DEVELOPMENT AGENCY

The U.S. Trade and Development Agency promotes American
products in emerging markets, primarily in South Africa, Thailand,
and Croatia (though it offers support throughout the world).
The agency "works closely with the Department of Commerce,
the Export-Import Bank, and the Overseas Private Investment
Corporation in funding various forms of technical assistance, fea-
sibility studies, training, orientation visits and business workshops
that support the development of a modern infrastructure and a fair
and open trading environment."

## U.S. INTERNATIONAL TRADE COMMISSION

The U.S. International Trade Commission advises both the executive branch and Congress about the impact of imports on American
industry, the remedies we should take against unfair trade practices, and the maintenance of our Harmonized Tariff Schedule.

## U.S. COURT OF INTERNATIONAL TRADE

Nine judges preside over the U.S. Court of International Trade.
The president (with the approval of the Senate) appoints these

judges to serve for life. Their role is to address all civil actions that relate to our imports and exports. The court has both national and international jurisdiction.

## THE EXPORT-IMPORT BANK OF THE UNITED STATES

The "EXIM" Bank provides export finance programs to American exporters in an effort to help make them more competitive overseas. These programs include working capital loans, loan repayment guarantees, loans to foreign purchasers of U.S. goods and services, and credit insurance. "The Bank focuses on exports to developing countries, aggressively countering trade subsidies of other governments, stimulating small business transactions, promoting the export of environmentally beneficial goods and services, and expanding project finance capabilities."

## U.S. AGENCY FOR INTERNATIONAL DEVELOPMENT

The U.S. Agency for International Development (USAID) distributes American aid throughout the world:

USAID attempts to further US foreign policy objectives by supporting the following: economic growth, international trade, agriculture, global health, democracy, and conflict and humanitarian assistance. The agency receives guidance from the State Department and collaborates with 3,500 US companies, universities, and voluntary organizations. USAID organizes missions to developing and least developed countries, oriented toward increasing their access to trade by promoting investment and building trade infrastructure.

## THE OVERSEAS PRIVATE INVESTMENT CORPORATION

The function of the Overseas Private Investment Corporation is to stimulate investment in developing markets and encourage the

creation of American jobs through U.S. investment overseas. The
agency provides loans, loan guarantees, and risk insurance. It also
works to increase awareness of overseas opportunities for small and
medium-sized businesses.

## SMALL BUSINESS ADMINISTRATION

The Small Business Administration offers counseling, training,
and legal assistance to help small businesses succeed in foreign
markets. To administer these services, it runs U.S. Export Centers
around the country.

## A VERY CROWDED TABLE

As you can see, a tremendous number of government agencies have
a role in our trade planning. That's an awful lot of voices and, one
would imagine, an awful lot of wrangling for turf. As you have
probably also noticed, there is a considerable amount of overlap in
the functions of these agencies as they relate to international commerce. What is most confounding is that no one agency oversees
all the others. This leads to an extraordinary waste of American tax
dollars and very high levels of inefficiency.

Unfortunately, the latest move regarding global commerce by
the federal government is not toward streamlining. In his first
State of the Union address, on January 27, 2010, President Obama
announced the National Export Initiative, the purpose of which
was to double exports in the next five years, generating two million new jobs. His executive order on March 11, 2010, included
the following:

> The economic and financial crisis has led to the loss of millions
> of U.S. jobs, and while the economy is beginning to show signs
> of recovery, millions of Americans remain unemployed or under-
> employed. Creating jobs in the United States and ensuring a

return to sustainable economic growth is the top priority for my Administration. A critical component of stimulating economic growth in the United States is ensuring that U.S. businesses can actively participate in international markets by increasing their exports of goods, services, and agricultural products. Improved export performance will, in turn, create good high-paying jobs.

The National Export Initiative (NEI) shall be an Administration initiative to improve conditions that directly affect the private sector's ability to export. The NEI will help meet my Administration's goal of doubling exports over the next 5 years by working to remove trade barriers abroad, by helping firms—especially small businesses—overcome the hurdles to entering new export markets, by assisting with financing, and in general by pursuing a Government-wide approach to export advocacy abroad, among other steps.[3]

That the Obama administration has prioritized global commerce is very good. However, the president has chosen to do so by layering more bureaucracy on top of a system already laden with bureaucracy (as this chapter has shown). The executive order establishes an Export Promotion Cabinet that consists of fourteen cabinet members as well as "the heads of other executive branch departments, agencies, and offices as the President may, from time to time, designate." As I write this, twenty-two people are serving on this cabinet—twenty-two powerful people with different fiefdoms. The odds are overwhelming that this is simply going to lead to gridlock and endless negotiation. The president has announced that we are going to double exports in the next five years, but his first step toward reaching that goal is to make a muddled system even more complicated and confusing.

Meanwhile, our chief competitors operate with stunning efficiency. Sun Tzu's *The Art of War* is required reading for senior diplomats and trade negotiators of the Ministry of Commerce of the People's Republic of China. Japan's enormous trade surpluses with the United States over the past thirty years are the result of relent-less planning and execution by Japan's omnipresent bureaucracy, in close association with its *kireitsu* (business conglomerates). Our competitors have armies of lawyers and trade specialists working feverishly to clear away barriers to their exports. Meanwhile, we have multiple agencies, most of them understaffed, to serve a por-tion of this role. Gross violations affecting thousands of American jobs go unchallenged, allowing foreign governments to trample American interests with impunity.

We must break out of our self-induced stupor and realize that we are competing not against foreign manufacturers in the inter-national marketplace, but against their governments. Essentially, our underfunded and ill-equipped small and medium-sized busi-nesses are doing battle against the governments of Brazil, China, India, Japan, South Korea, and the other countries that contribute to our record-level trade deficit.

Our approach to organizing government involvement in our global entrepreneurial efforts mirrors what seems to be our overall governmental attitude toward international commerce: it is impor-tant enough to warrant some attention but not nearly important enough for us to marshal our forces in an all-out effort to succeed. This message rings resoundingly in the ears of our most critical trading partners. They know we don't take international trade as seriously as they do. Therefore, they know they can tilt the playing field in their direction.

For Conscientious Equity to have any chance of becoming the new paradigm in the international community, America must lead the way. To do so, we must reorganize our government's administra-tion of global commerce—and in a dramatic fashion. Our exports have a profound impact on the American economy, America's security, and the values we prize so greatly. We must, therefore, announce to the world that we consider the business we do with our trading partners to be at least as important as transportation, energy, housing and urban development, and veterans' affairs, all of which have streamlined departments within the executive branch. In other words, we need to create a Department of Global Commerce headed by a secretary of global commerce who has extensive experience in international business, and we must give this department the ultimate power in making trade policy recommendations to the president.

The role of the secretary of global commerce would be substantially different from the current roles of the U.S. trade representative and the U.S. secretary of commerce. This cabinet member would preside over all American trade policy discussion. The Trade Policy Review Group and the Trade Policy Staff Committee are bureaucratic bodies that stand in the way of clarifying objectives. The secretary of global trade would of course receive input from other departments and agencies, but he would outrank the heads of other departments in matters of global commerce. This would make the position exponentially stronger than the current position of USTR and, therefore, tremendously more attractive to fill and effective to execute. All agencies that are focused today on commerce and trade would be consolidated into the Department of Global Commerce. The cost savings would be enormous and could be reinvested into the hiring of lawyers and other staff needed to do battle with our competitors in enforcing agreements. This would cost the taxpayer nothing but would be a tremendous asset in opening foreign markets to American products and services. It would also play a vital role in the negotiation and execution of our future Conscientious Equity Accords.

One would think that we might have considered such a position necessary around the time we enacted the Marshall Plan. Certainly, one would think that we would have moved to streamline our bureaucracy during the seventies, when we first started to amass significant trade deficits. As we have seen even in national security matters, however, we are extremely slow to recognize that too many cooks in the kitchen turn out a lumpy and unsavory broth.

If we were waiting for a crisis to fix the problem, the crisis already exists: an eight hundred billion dollar trade deficit. If we were looking for a new idea to supplant the outworn ideas we have been employing with regard to international commerce, we have one we can all rally behind: Conscientious Equity. Perhaps this is the message our leaders have been waiting to hear. Perhaps, until now, they somehow believed that we were rich enough to allow for gross inefficiencies in the way we did business with other countries and that we could use other methods to address issues such as poverty, hunger, corruption, the environment, and human rights abuses. Perhaps, with the common sense and moral imperative inherent in Conscientious Equity, they will see that it is no longer okay to regard global commerce as an afterthought and to relegate its management to a hodgepodge of governmental organizations.

We are long past the need for a Department of Global Commerce. If we are going to bring Conscientious Equity to the world, it is essential that we have one.

## CHAPTER TWELVE

# I'D LOVE TO CHANGE THE WORLD . . .

I HAVE ALWAYS BEEN A DREAMER. I acquired this trait at an early age, and it has sustained and guided me throughout my life. As far back as I can remember, I set big goals for myself and worked hard to meet them.

One of my first memories is of playing football. I played whenever and wherever I could, even in our small living room when the weather would not cooperate. I urged my father to throw the ball far in front of me so I would have to leap headlong to catch it. When there was no one to play with, I could entertain myself for hours rifling the ball at imaginary targets on a wild cherry tree in our front yard. I scrambled to the cheers of a thunderous stadium sequestered in my eight-year-old head. The experience became real when I played my heart out on intramural and high school fields. Bruised and bleeding with a mouth full of dirt, I gave one hundred percent. It felt good.

My next passion struck me at fourteen. As I sat in my high school music class, the modulation of chords played slowly and deliberately on the piano by my music teacher blew me away. He tested us on our ability to differentiate between major or minor chords. At first, I found the task easy, but it got harder when the teacher began striking inverted chords. I closed my eyes to concentrate on the simple but captivating sounds emanating from the spruce soundboard. With each chord, I imagined stories intertwined with landscapes. I was hooked. I knew I had to learn everything I could about this mesmerizing instrument.

My parents bought me an old upright piano, on which I practiced for endless hours. If I were to realize my dream to be a music man, I first had to make it into music school. My father drove me to Rowan State University in southern New Jersey for my audition. I was so nervous that I could hardly feel my fingers. Somehow I got through my pieces, and a few weeks later I received an acceptance letter. This was my first big accomplishment in life. I had set a personal goal, and I met it.

My university days are a complete haze to me. Not because of weeks of drunken debauchery, although I must confess there was some of that, but because, for me to keep up with my fellow students, I had to work ten times harder. The school was home to so many incredibly talented kids pursuing dreams of music. Most of them were child prodigies, who had studied music since they were small children, and whose parents and grandparents were professional musicians. While I was doing drills and calisthenics to harden my body to play football, they were doing Hannon piano exercises to make their fingers fly. But I persevered because my art filled me with passion.

Music and sports taught me to never give up and that perfection
is in the nuances. To achieve perfection takes nothing less than
total concentration and dedication. I had to be prepared to make
huge sacrifices for my passion and practice the rudiments of my
craft until they became second nature. This formula ultimately led
me to the passion that has been at the center of my professional life:
entrepreneurialism.

At the beginning of this book, I told you about my first full-time
job. I'd like to go back to that now to tell one of the formative stories of my life. My boss and mentor, Hugo Garin, was an incredible
man. He and his wife, Monica, escaped communism under the
most difficult of circumstances. Fluent in seven languages, Hugo
was an engineer, a designer, and a natural salesman. He was a true
citizen of the world who had a never-ending repertoire of spell-
binding stories. Each night at dinner he held court. I wanted more
than anything to be like him one day.

Hugo's boss, John, was a dour British executive in prim bowties
and thick blue pinstriped suits who spoke the Queen's English in
long, drawn-out sentences. He seemed to me to have a way of making things much more complicated than they actually were. In my
naive estimation, John was a nice man, but I did not think that his
intellectual skills matched Hugo's.

After one of my meetings with John and Hugo, I found myself
alone with Hugo for a few moments. Full of piss and vinegar and
perpetually in a hurry to hit the byways of Southeast Asia and
dig up sales opportunities, I remarked to Hugo with disdain and
mischief that *he* should be John's boss. In a low voice, I leaned over
Hugo's shoulder and added, "After all, John is a glorified wimp
who does not deserve to be leading us."

I was knocked off my feet by Hugo's reaction to my obvious
impertinence: he told me that my mind was nothing but "meaningless mush." I left his office with my tail between my legs and
dreaded a follow-up meeting a few days later, where I expected

one of his patented thrashings. Instead, he imparted to me the most profound wisdom I have ever heard. Without this conversation, I would not be where I am today. He admonished me to keep in mind that youth and hard work were not enough to ensure success. In his thick Eastern European accent, he chastised, "You have no idea the decisions that John needs to make every day and the burdens that are solely his. He stands alone dealing with pressures that would break most men. Any escape he has lasts only a fleeting moment. He has his times of triumph, but they quickly pass. His problems are endless and his frustrations deep, dark, and omnipresent."

Leaning across his desk, with his gray eyes exploding behind his signature thick, black-rimmed glasses, Hugo said, "Do not think for one second that you are tough enough to be in John's shoes. What you need to figure out from this day forward is will you *ever* be tough enough?"

Over the years, "tough enough" came to mean many things to me. It meant the mental strength to deal with the pressure akin to being one hundred and eighty feet beneath the ocean's surface. You wonder if you have enough air in your tank to make it to the surface. Do you have the will to fight?

Toughness means having the wherewithal to go toe-to-toe against your European, Japanese, and Chinese competitors to win business that is essential to our American factories and workers. You take the fight to these competitors knowing that there are barriers to your success. You fight knowing that, whereas U.S. government support for American exports is waning, most foreign governments aggressively offer everything their exporters need. It doesn't take long to realize that, as an American international entrepreneur, you wake up each day recreating the film "High Noon"—it's just you against all comers, and you are outnumbered and lack resources.

Toughness also means accepting that your entrepreneurial dream will always consume more capital and take longer than you anticipate. There will be countless lonely days and nights when the only resource you can count on having is your passion. America's twenty-seven million small business owners share this vigil. Each day, we go to work to sustain our piece of the American dream. We don't get parades. There's no "Small Business Appreciation Day." Heck, the president barely even acknowledges small business. But we're out there. We've always been out there. We're doing the heavy lifting for our economy, and we hold the key to recovering from our current economic malaise. Energizing small business and entrepreneurialism is essential to a world with Conscientious Equity. Each day we face daunting challenges. Yet we prevail without public complaint. We have long ago stopped looking for government support. Of the recent stimulus package, approximately *one percent* went to support the people that have been responsible for more than seventy percent of our job growth over the last decade. That's what makes the American entrepreneur so tough . . . and resilient. They do more with less.

I have discussed at great length in this book my concept of Conscientious Equity. As I slogged through the battlefields of trade, I came to realize that Conscientious Equity was a rare commodity. I found myself staring down the barriers, manipulations, and distortions that Americans must encounter to sell our products. I was appalled by the discrimination and theft openly practiced by foreign governments against our entrepreneurs and exporters. Raised in the United States, where fair play is a guiding principle, I was sickened by the redistribution of wealth away from our country to prop up corrupt foreign governments and their crony corporations.

In the fabric of my soul, I knew that there had to be a better way to move forward and that finding that way meant personally addressing the ills that plague the world. I knew that I could not stand by idly witnessing the great social ills of poverty, corruption, and the rape of our planet. I had to apply the same passion

I devoted to building my entrepreneurial dream to speaking out against these scourges and to spreading the word of Conscientious Equity, which I believe is a true game changer.

The American dream was founded on the ideal that if you worked hard and were inventive, you could succeed. Entrepreneurs grew their enterprises, and millions of jobs were created. Their success spawned thousands of other entrepreneurs, who also built successful companies. Anything seemed possible. Today, there is a growing sense of disillusionment, a feeling that the American dream is no longer within reach. Millions of Americans are rudderless, seeking some direction to give their lives meaning. Increasingly, there is no longer a compass, such as once rested in the hands of the federal government, that provides encouragement to pursue new enterprises. American workers have become the "marginalized majority" by a political process that has deserted them. Millions of citizens are sitting on the sidelines, waiting to get into the entrepreneurial game, but real and perceived roadblocks in their way intimidate them.

It is time to restore America's belief that this country's best times are still ahead and that there is a role for everyone. No nation on earth can outthink or outwork us. What is missing is a comprehensive, principled belief system that gets Americans back to work, creating wealth for themselves and our country, by unleashing their huge reservoir of creativity, dedication, and hard work. By letting Americans be Americans, we not only help ourselves but also provide the inspiration to uplift countless millions in every corner of the world who are trapped in misery without hope. By creating an atmosphere of hope, we can help ensure sustained growth for the expansion of free enterprise and entrepreneurialism by dealing head-on with the destabilizing curse of poverty; its sinister enabler, corruption; and the devastation of environmental rape.

Americans must embrace Conscientious Equity as the future of this country and take responsibility for playing an active role in shaping how America sustains free enterprise and economic growth. That means a vision for a strong, vibrant America leading the world in adopting the tenets of Conscientious Equity. I truly believe that this is the only way to bring together the citizens of all nations in the mutual pursuit of a better world.

Part of our responsibility is to make our government representatives accountable for their performance. When they remain loyal to a political party to curry favor with party leaders and ignore the consequences of ill-advised programs and bills that have a negative impact on their constituents, their behavior perverts the reason they were elected as our representatives. The welfare of the nation should be the overriding priority. Those who fail to recognize their responsibility do so at their own political peril. Conscientious Equity demands that we pay attention to the issues that affect this nation. To feign ignorance is to shirk one's responsibility as a citizen, and to ignore the issues constitutes a failure of moral character.

Our founding fathers always envisioned an America where every citizen had equal opportunity and equal protection. They recognized the challenge and took action by creating the greatest governing document in history: the U.S. Constitution. It is time to harness the principles and power of that great document and restore the American dream to every citizen.

I say to social agencies that the time is *now* to stop ignoring the dehumanizing manacles of poverty. Rhetorical indignation alone will make no difference. Conscientious Equity does not tolerate the status quo when the status quo is broken. First, we must deal head-on with that sinister enabler of poverty, corruption. We should no longer allow despotic rulers to use riches made from trade with America to trample their people. Instead, we need to give other nations a taste of democracy by allowing American entrepreneurs to freely travel and trade with the world. As an American entrepreneur, I have personally provided resources and guidance to countless entrepreneurs in developing countries to realize their dreams of beginning businesses. This effort must be multiplied a million times. The only losers in a world embracing Conscientious Equity will be dictators, their cronies, and the poverty that their corrupt practices perpetuate.

I say to the labor unions that Conscientious Equity demands that workers everywhere are entitled to safe working conditions that respect their dignity. If they choose to form unions, they should be allowed to do so, but only through the sanctity of the secret ballot. No government can be allowed to abuse its workforce to gain a competitive advantage for its manufacturers. Conscientious Equity recognizes that American workers are some of the most competitive and productive in the world, even though the world trading system is corrupt and skewed against them. The solution is not the high tariffs and isolationism of the Smoot-Hawley Tariff Act of 1929 but tearing down the walls that prevent Americans from being successful. If we are successful, we lift up people everywhere. Conscientious Equity rests on the belief in the goodness of America, its entrepreneurs, and its workers. This goodness must be set free upon the world, where it will mean not only more and better paying jobs in the United States, but also for laborers everywhere. We cannot live in a world where one side always wins and the other always loses.

I say to environmental groups that Conscientious Equity not only insists on codifying in law real environmental protections that are comprehensive and applicable to everyone, but also that we provide the resources and resolve to enforce them. No nation should be able to plunder the earth and poison the environment to gain economic advantage. Any nation benefiting from a global trading system that creates wealth and jobs has the moral responsibility to all nations to protect our planet. Environmental abuse knows no national boundary. The loss of a rain forest, the extinction of a species, the creation of man-made deserts through desiccation, and the contamination high in our atmosphere and in our rivers, lakes, and seas pose enormous threats for us all. Conscientious Equity finally provides a basis from which to manage our world's precious but fragile environment.

There have been millions of dreamers before me, and there will be millions more to come. From my dream of a better world for all of us, for all citizens of all nations, have come the immutable truths of Conscientious Equity—a world trading system that respects free enterprise, entrepreneurialism, and the right of humanity to live in a better world. However, it will only happen if we are all tough enough to make it happen.

The great blues rocker Alvin Lee once sang, "I'd love to change the world...but I don't know what to do." To him, and to all of you, I respond, "I'd love to change the world...and I *do* know what to do." I know we can change the world with Conscientious Equity.

# SOME STOPS ON THE WORLD TOUR

MY GOAL WITH THIS BOOK has been to start a conversation—a conversation that snowballs into an international movement. Conscientious Equity is not an idea hatched in a think tank. It is an idea born from decades of interaction and enterprise with people all over the planet. From this interaction comes my steadfast belief that the ideals I am most concerned about achieving with Conscientious Equity are truly universal: that everyone should have the chance to make a decent living; to enjoy freedom from hunger, poverty, and corruption; and to live in an environment sustainable for future generations. As I have stated elsewhere in this book, just because a concept might be universal does not mean that the manifestation of that concept is the same everywhere. This world's cultures are remarkably diverse.

Understanding and embracing this truth is essential if we are going to make Conscientious Equity work. Here, frankly, is where Americans have a tendency to fall woefully short. As has almost certainly become clear by now, I am a deeply patriotic man who takes great pride in his country. No one would ever mistake me for anything other than an American. Still, my love of the American way of life does not extend to ignoring all other ways of life. Sadly, too many Americans put on blinders when it comes to the ways that people from other nations think and interact. This is simply not advisable when dealing with today's world. If I have at all convinced you to take the concept of Conscientious Equity seriously, then, surely, you understand that we cannot make this work unless we understand the needs and mores of those with whom we share the planet.

Although we are a nation of immigrants, we tend to be culturally illiterate. Until we let go of our parochial sensibilities and venture to understand the nuances and needs of other cultures, we will never be able to fully embrace Conscientious Equity. The very notion of Conscientious Equity requires us to appreciate that each of us—no matter where we are from in the world—has a stake in the future we are creating.

I present the pages that follow as a bit of a primer. There is not nearly enough space in this book to offer a comprehensive view at the wide range of cultural differences in the world. Nor do I claim to be any sort of expert with regard to these cultural differences. However, I have been traveling the globe for decades, and I have lived in cultures very different from ours.

Without any braggadocio, I think that today's entrepreneurs have a direct link back to the eighteenth and nineteenth centuries, when schooners and clipper ships traversed the globe to open trade routes. When they returned and shared what they had seen of other lands and cultures, they were often described as "men of the world." Despite the risks of their forays, these men shared a passionate wanderlust and a keen sense of natural curiosity about the world. Today's entrepreneurs must embrace the adventurous, risk-taking spirit of their forebears. We inherently understand that the greater the risk, the greater the opportunity to develop new markets and revenue. Being a man of the world is a proud tradition in American culture, and the term often shows up in American literature. Mark Twain, in *A Tramp Abroad*, wrote, "I had hardly begun my work when a tall, slender, vigorous American youth of about twenty-three, who was on his way down the mountain, entered and came toward me with that breezy self-complacency which is the adolescent's idea of the well-bred ease of the man of the world."

In a sense, I do consider myself a man of the world—not because I have done anything extraordinary but because, as an American entrepreneur, I was willing to face head on any contingency or uncertainty that arose. By reaching into the unknown, learning to live outside my comfort zone, and conquering my fears, I was able to gain firsthand knowledge of both the good and the evil of many world cultures. Entrepreneurs who fail to open themselves to the vast variety of viewpoints across the globe will miss out on creating invaluable transactions and interactions.

The Age of Discovery was fueled by trade. It was a time when brave men commanding great sailing ships equipped with the crudest of technology explored and mapped the world. I am humbled to think I am heir to their profession.

In the lobby of my office hang four large maps published in 1775 by Tobias Conrad Lotter, one of the most respected cartographers of his time. These maps fascinate me for many reasons. Even though it would be decades until the interiors of the Asian, African, and South American continents would be explored or mapped, by 1775 their perimeters were already clearly defined. Lotter was unable to map at the time the western North American continent; he simply left it blank.

I am certain that our founding fathers would have studied these and similar maps at great length. Such maps would have been the center of much debate and speculation as they plotted the course of our young, fledgling nation. Whether they were in Boston, New York, or Philadelphia, when George Washington, John Adams, and Thomas Jefferson gazed west beyond the Ohio and Mississippi rivers, they might as well have been looking at the moon.

An unexplored, unknown North American continent was the genesis of the United States. It gave rise to the American spirit and to American free enterprise and entrepreneurship. This was the foundation of the American dream that George Washington, John Adams, and Thomas Jefferson understood. In fact, Washington, himself a cartographer, fervently believed that the future of the United States lay westward, out in the uncharted territories.

From our very beginning as a nation, Americans ventured into the unknown and conquered their fears. They brought with them their passion, their dreams, and their ingenuity as they worked to make a better life for their families and those who came after.

Today's America desperately needs to rediscover this spirit of venturing out into the unknown. This thirst, this core belief, omnipresent at our nation's beginning and now safely sequestered deep in our souls, will create the jobs and generate the wealth that will keep our country and our world strong, vibrant, and healthy.

Through the prism of my experiences as an entrepreneur and man of the world, I have become acquainted with several cultures. The anecdotes that follow may help readers gain an understanding of why the countries I discuss operate the way they do today and how their customs have evolved. I offer these glimpses as an observer, not to pass judgment on governments or customs.

## Beverly Hills East

American entrepreneurs have been salivating at the size of the Chinese market for decades, just waiting for the opportunity to sell their goods to a consumer group that numbers 1.3 billion. While that market has yet to materialize for reasons I will touch on in a moment, perhaps the most encouraging news for exporters is the high demand for luxury goods in China today. Although high-quality knockoffs are openly available at a fraction of the cost, numerous Chinese consumers want the real thing and won't settle for anything less.

It is anticipated the Chinese will soon surpass the Japanese as the largest consumers of luxury brands. The 2010 Wealth Report from the Hurun Research Institute puts the number of Chinese millionaires at eight hundred and seventy-five thousand and notes that each owns an average of three luxury cars and four high-end watches. A fascinating insight as to where China may be heading is how luxury goods, fashion, and fine dining are combining to further distance China from its Communist past.

I recently enjoyed an evening in Shanghai at Three on the Bund. This is a multistory shopping, dining, and entertainment complex in one of the city's beautiful, historic buildings that was originally constructed in 1916. A Taiwanese company leased the building, brought in a well-known American architect, and spent millions to turn it into an oasis of pure decadence. Chairman Mao is rolling over in his grave.

It is not just the foreign community that enjoys the offerings of Three on the Bund. Upwardly mobile Chinese are well represented in its nightly clientele, where an evening out can set them back the equivalent of what, for an average Chinese worker, would be several months' salary.

On the ground floor are elegant boutiques, including the China flagship store of Giorgio Armani. Located in the building is the luxurious Evian Spa, described on their website as "a chic, clean and contemporary escape from the bustle and stress of the city streets below." This was Evian's first spa outside of France. There are three upscale dining establishments, including a French restaurant that offers two-thousand-dollar bottles of wine. There is a great nightclub overlooking the Manhattan-esque skyline of Pudong, staffed by bartenders imported from France who create a drink that involves lighting the entire bar on fire. The lines for the nightclub can get long, and you can wait forever to get in if you don't have the right connections.

This Shanghai complex is a clear sign of an evolving culture. If you recall my story in chapter 1 about peering into mainland China from Hong Kong, you will know that it would have been nearly inconceivable to me at that point that the feudal landscape I saw would soon be the home of nearly a million millionaires.

Still, the notion of China being a nation of 1.3 billion consumers is misleading. You can subtract nine hundred million of these people immediately, as they are rural peasants whose lives have not changed much for centuries. They have no access to jobs, education, or health care, let alone luxury goods. They are dirt poor and barely scratch out a living. The 2004 per capita income of farm workers in China was the equivalent of just three hundred and twenty-four dollars per year. Sixty percent of China's labor force works in the agricultural sector. These folks are not going to be purchasing much of anything for a long, long time to come.

That leaves four hundred million people, which is nearly equal to the combined population of the United States, Canada, and Mexico. Again, one must examine the numbers. China's average per capita income in 2009 was about six thousand six hundred dollars. Although there has been some progress in reducing extreme poverty, China's annual per capita income growth still lags behind its annual GDP growth. Getting reliable data on income groups in

China is very difficult. Only sketchy information is available from government agencies, and that information is always skewed for publicity purposes to highlight China's economic success. Some studies suggest that as much as nineteen percent of China's population is "middle income," more commonly called "middle strata." There is no official or widely accepted definition for this term, but outside analysts loosely define it as households earning more than five thousand dollars a year. Even if you consider that money goes much farther in China than it does in America, the reality is that the vast majority of this middle income group is in fact made up of the working poor. It will be decades before this nineteen percent becomes active consumers. My experiences in China have shown me, though, that the country is evolving so quickly that it is nearly impossible to predict where its culture will go next.

## THE GREAT WALL OF JAPAN

Perhaps no other country is as engraved on the American psyche as Japan. World War II left a deep scar on America's perceptions of this country, which lingered for years. Although these wounds have healed, we still have mixed feelings about Japan's impact on the American economy.

The taxi route to my Tokyo hotel takes me through Hibiya Park, to the front gates of the Imperial Palace. We drive around the palace's moat and incredible walls then past the Diet (Parliament) Building. Here, Emperor Hirohito gave his approval to the war plans that caused so much pain—from the attack on Pearl Harbor on December 7, 1941, to the fall of Bataan and Corregidor in April and May 1942 until Japan's unconditional surrender on September 2, 1945. It is at the Diet that Prime Minister Hideki Tojo ordered his generals to have no mercy on the American prisoners of war and the "inferior" races that the Japanese were rapidly and brutally conquering. Today, we occasionally still witness anti-Japanese demonstrations in China and South Korea that are full of raw emotion over wartime atrocities.

Emperor Hirohito was an important participant in Japan's policies leading up to and during World War II. Documented research by historians now largely rejects one of the notions pervasive after the war: that Japan's ministers and generals had duped him into actively participating in this decision making and the atrocities and war crimes that resulted from it. In the half-century since the war, we have learned that General McArthur and the American occupation authorities invented the fiction of Emperor Hirohito as victim immediately after the surrender to save him from the war crimes tribunal and the certainty of a death sentence. At the time, the only thing the Japanese political elite and militarists hated more than the Americans were the Communists. The political elite's power and control—its very reason to exist—emanated directly from the emperor. It was therefore imperative to reinvent the emperor as a mechanism to control the defeated and demoralized Japanese people and, thus, prevent Japan from degenerating into civil war, resulting in a real possibility of their falling to Communist control. This background set the stage for America's fiercest enemy to become one of its most trusted and important allies.

A former vice admiral of the U.S. Seventh Fleet stationed at Yokosuka, Japan, reminded me at a recent dinner party of the importance of Japanese-American relations when I complained about how difficult it is to export American products to Japan. I asked him why we allowed such unfair trade practices. He quickly shot back that the American-Japanese relationship was like a three-legged stool, with political, military, and economic legs. On the political and military side of things, Japan was indispensable. The Japanese were supportive of and major contributors to America's efforts to maintain peace and prosperity in Asia. If we had to turn a blind eye on the economic side, this was an acceptable price to pay, considering the benefits that we—and much of the world—derived.

As an American exporter, I do not subscribe to the vice admiral's point of view on the trade issue, but I fully appreciate the complexities and importance of the American-Japanese alliance in today's world. I have been searching over the past several years for an explanation for my frustrations as an American exporter. I only recently realized why I wasn't getting any closer to an answer: I had been looking in the wrong place. To find the reasons I was seeking, I needed to look deep into the subconscious of a nation.

When General MacArthur rehabilitated Emperor Hirohito, he learned something that everyone doing business in Japan needs to understand but very few ever do. The emperor sits at the top of an intricate system. The government and bureaucracy come just beneath him. Then follow the large Japanese corporations; then, their subcompanies; and then, finally, the people.

Japanese society resembles Mt. Fuji, the symbol of Japan. At the top is the beautiful volcanic, snow-covered cone that represents the emperor, followed by the bureaucracy and the *keiretsu* in the middle, and the people at its base. From the outside, the structure looks sturdy and imposing, but, on the inside, it is empty.

This inner emptiness has a significant impact on the Japanese people themselves. The effect of this emptiness is something like a terrifying event that took place in one's life that one blocks from one's mind. One creates emptiness to replace the trauma, even though one cannot erase the impact of the trauma on one's life.

To fill up this emptiness among the Japanese people, an elaborate system, exclusive to Japan, has evolved over many centuries. This system governs all aspects of life, society, and business and requires strict adherence, without which it would crumble. Adherence means allowing oneself to be absorbed into the system and to not stand out as an individual. Foreigners (non-Japanese) automatically stand out as they have individuality. Therefore, allowing foreigners into the system would lead to its destruction. This has made Japan the most homogeneous country in the world, with less than one percent of the population being non-Japanese. Because entrepreneurialism is a form of individuality, Japanese society discourages it.

The Japanese, I have observed, tend to refer to their company colleagues not by name, but by the positions they hold. The organization is always more important than the individual. To survive, everyone must find, and then hold onto, a place where they fit in. Japanese executives receive promotions not because of performance, creativity, and risk taking but because of their ability to maintain the system. This kind of blind loyalty and sacrifice has helped companies such as Toyota, Canon, and Sony to manufacture some of the highest-quality products in the world. This approach to doing business makes the trains run on time. However, it also allows some of the world's most inefficient industries—such as Japan's agriculture, construction materials, communications, food service, and retail industries—to exist without improvement. The Japanese instinctively maintain a system that keeps foreign competition out and dutifully purchase locally made products even when they are overpriced and inferior.

An important feature of the Japanese system is the ceremony. From the low bows to the way executives exchange business cards with two hands, ceremony is omnipresent. On a recent trip to Tokyo, I purchased a train ticket from a machine. An animated character appeared on the screen thanking me with a proper bow. From an American perspective, it is easy to look at such ceremony as a case of form being more important than substance, but it is important to the Japanese. I deal with this conflict regularly in my business dealings in Japan. For example, I recently had to make a slight change to a meeting time with a senior Japanese executive in Nagoya. He curtly dismissed the idea and said, "Perhaps we should not meet at all since you are *so busy.*" I had just traveled halfway around the world and gone through considerable expense to get there, yet he was intransigent. In his mind, I had disrespected the ceremony.

In a different kind of ceremony, I have engaged in all-night working sessions with Japanese contractors to get documentation completed and quotations finalized for large construction projects. In the course of the session, it quickly becomes apparent that the only point of staying up until sunrise is to show how tough and dedicated one is. At a certain point, productivity drops to a trickle. It is the ritual of taking oneself to the limit of one's endurance that is important, not the actual results of the many hours.

As these examples demonstrate, preparation and ceremony are critical in doing business in Japan. What we may consider insignificant, silly, or superficial is part of the fabric that holds Japan together.

I have learned to view everything in Japan in the context of the country's unique system. Doing so has helped me to understand why the Japanese reject foreigners and their products so completely. Why do the Japanese cling so frantically to their inefficiencies and overpriced goods? Because, right now, they believe they cannot exist without them.

## Igniting a Light for Entrepreneurialism

Being an international entrepreneur means being prepared for anything. Although acquainting yourself with the local culture is critical, sometimes it isn't enough. Sometimes, the culture is in such turmoil that the ground seems to be shifting beneath you.

In 1989, at the beginning of an economic boom throughout most of Southeast Asia that would last nearly a decade, I established a manufacturing facility in the Philippines to produce stainless steel commercial food-service equipment. As an entrepreneur with a grand vision and limited resources, I found an old, dilapidated warehouse in metropolitan Manila for my factory. The roof leaked, nearly every window was shattered, the restrooms had an awful smell that made your eyes water, and the floors were so uneven that simply walking around the office could make you dizzy.

My job was made much more complex because the opening of my factory collided with one of its darkest moments in the history of the Philippines. Still reeling from the upheaval of the People Power Revolution, the country faced massive civil unrest, exacerbated by frequent right-wing coups attempts and the omnipresent threat of communist insurgents.

This was just the beginning, however. The communists, who were openly hostile toward management and practiced extortion for their personal gain, infiltrated the labor unions. The labor unions made it impossible to predictably produce anything because of their continuous threat of strikes, work slowdowns, and sabotage. There was corruption everywhere, at every level of society. It wasn't long before this destabilization eroded the fabric of the country and the quality of life there. Opportunity was replaced by oppressive poverty, and the infrastructure eroded to the point that there were daily random power outages that lasted several hours. The government referred to these as brownouts, but there was nothing brown about them. Without electricity, it was pitch black, and work at our plant came to a standstill. My job was to manage chaos, which was never in short supply.

As I learned to navigate through these challenges, I got a call summoning me to an important briefing at the American Embassy, a meeting that would shake my world. At the meeting, I learned that negotiations were going poorly between the U.S. and Philippine governments on the future status of the American military bases at Clark Airfield and Subic Bay. Recognizing a weakened American presence, communist insurgents safely encamped deep in the jungles of Luzon had begun sending "Sparrow Units" to Manila to assassinate Americans. Sparrow Units were small cells that were heavily armed and trained in hit-and-run tactics. The Communist Party wanted to intimidate Americans so that the United States would vacate the despised bases. As I was a high-profile business-man married to a well-known Filipino actress, I was believed to be a target.

The CIA officer in charge of security at the embassy spoke in a somber voice as he warned me to prepare myself for whatever eventuality might come. I was a marked man. I was to change my route and the times I traveled each day. I had to avoid crowds and traffic jams. (I never figured out how staying out of traffic jams was remotely possible, considering how congested Manila's streets were. Telling me to stop the lava flows coming off Mt. Pinatubo would have been more feasible.) I always had to be alert and watch for anything out of the ordinary. They told me to keep a low profile (difficult, given how the press covered my wife). I was forced to post security around-the-clock armed security personnel at my factory with twelve-gauge sawed-off shotguns and to live in a heavily guarded compound. One of my most vivid memories of this period is arriving at the plant each day to the crisp military a solutes of my guards. I lived like a prisoner, yet my only "crime" was being an entrepreneur and creating desperately needed jobs.

One evening, as I sat in the backseat of my SUV on my way home, with my driver zigzagging through the streets of Manila, I came to the realization that I had tried to suppress the one emotion that should have been natural during this entire ordeal: I was scared. Eventually, every entrepreneur has a rendezvous with fear. This wasn't the fear of failure, though. It was a real fear for the safety and security of my family, my company, and myself.

Battling through my fears was especially important if I was going to make my Philippines operation as successful as I wanted it to be. McDonald's was a huge customer of ours, and the company's purchasing managers from several Asian countries scheduled a visit to our facilities during this crazy time. This was a very important gathering for my company, since it needed to get buy-in from these managers and persuade them to source their kitchens from our operation in the Philippines. McDonald's had legitimate concerns about whether my company could be a reliable vendor, as the Philippines was making daily world headlines for all the wrong reasons. McDonald's officials were concerned about the visit, too. One day, I got a call from a senior executive at the McDonald's headquarters in Oakbrook, Illinois, asking, "What can you do to guarantee our safety?"

When an entrepreneur is threatened with extinction, you can always bet on him or her to dig deep. I called my congressman and told him how this Pioneering Export Manufacturer (a distinction given to the company by the Philippine Board of Investments) was in trouble. He called the constabulary commander on our behalf, who promised police escorts everywhere I and my guests went during the McDonald's visit, as well as armed guards at all of our functions.

When the McDonald's team came to visit our manufacturing facility, I prayed that the power would stay on during these few hours. My employees and I were all in our positions awaiting their arrival. In the distance, I could hear the sirens of the McDonald's managers' motorcade making its final approach. Then, almost on cue, the power went off with a loud pop. My heart sank in the darkness, but my industrious staff was ready. Within moments, they had hundreds of candles burning throughout the offices and on the factory floor. We had hoped to project a different image, but the glow had quite an effect.

The McDonald's folks left the Philippines pleased with their visit. As a result, our business with them grew significantly, allowing us to add many new jobs. We had adapted on the fly. I had ventured out into the unknown and come away with something special.

## A Door of Gold and a Sword of Steel

America's relationship with the Middle East continues to be problematic, particularly with Arab countries, where our general lack of cultural understanding and their perceived role in supporting terrorism creates a gulf between the nations. Relating my personal experiences on the Arabian Peninsula is not intended to denigrate Arab customs, but rather to offer a perspective on building close relationships with business contacts that share a common quest to use trade and the principles of Conscientious Equity to help form a true partnership.

Of all the countries on the Arabian Peninsula, Saudi Arabia practices the strictest form of Islam: the state adheres to Wahhabism, a belief in the literal interpretation of the Koran and the absolute oneness of God. Everyone who does not follow the puritanical faith is considered a heathen or an idolater to be countered by jihad, or holy war. I experienced an example of this intolerance during one of my trips to Jeddah, when I visited a wealthy Saudi businessman's home. His villa, like those of many of his status, was a large walled compound, which included massive structures to house his extended family. It came equipped with a commercial-grade kitchen, where large quantities of food could be prepared to feed the many occupants and servants.

In the forecourt of this beautiful villa, a ten-foot-high, solid gold door was mounted prominently on one of the walls. This was at one time the entrance door of the Kaaba, the dark, cube-like building at the center of the Grand Mosque of Mecca. All Moslems pray in the direction of the Kaaba, and they know that one day they will be laid to face it in their graves. Moslems believe the Kaaba was built by Adam, destroyed by the Flood, and then rebuilt by Abraham and Ishmael. They consider it the most holy site in the world. It contains the black stone, the official starting point of the walk around the Kaaba that is the core of the hajj, the holy pilgrimage. The Prophet Muhammad is said to have kissed the black stone at the start of his hajj, and it has been held in awe since the founding of Islam. Scholars believe that the stone is actually a meteorite that was worshiped by nomadic Arabs for many centuries before Islam became the dominant religion of the area.

The king of Saudi Arabia replaces the gold door of the Kaaba every so often and gives the old door as a gift to an important supporter or member of the Islamic community. This is, obviously, a huge honor. My hosts told me about the gold door when I arrived at the villa and sternly warned me that Islamic law strictly forbade me from touching it. The warning prickled my senses in ways that I am sure my hosts never intended.

For professionals from the United States and other Western countries, working in Saudi Arabia can be financially rewarding, and life can be reasonably comfortable. Most Westerners live in walled, secure compounds, with swimming pools, tennis courts, and private schools. White-collar workers, however, represent a tiny minority of all the foreign workers in the kingdom. Because of the fantastic wealth of the small indigenous populations, which are imbued with clannish tribalism and nomadic traditions on the Arabian Peninsula, we see a very peculiar demographic.

Consider this: the six nations of the Gulf Cooperative Council— Bahrain, Kuwait, Oman, Qatar, Saudi Arabia, and the United Arab Emirates—have a total population of thirty-five million. Out of this, more than thirteen million are expatriates, most of whom are non-Arab foreign workers. In some instances, local citizens are in the minority in their own countries. Furthermore, seventy percent of the overall workforce is made up of foreigners, a fraction that increases to ninety percent in the private sector.

Saudi Arabia is, by far, the largest and most important country in the region. It has an overall population of twenty-four million, of which seven million are foreign workers. Saudis can be found at the senior levels of corporate ownership and management, but almost everyone else in the company is foreign. This makes for a unique experience when negotiating and doing business.

Many of Saudi Arabia's seven million foreign workers live under conditions that one could define as a form of slavery. (Saudi Arabia did not ban slavery until 1962.) The vast majority of these workers are from South Asia and are very poor. They often live in squalor, because they never receive the income their employers promised them. According to Human Rights Watch, these foreign laborers—nearly one-third of the kingdom's population—face torture, forced confessions, and unfair trails when accused of a crime. Every foreign worker must have a Saudi sponsor and cannot change jobs without the sponsor's permission. Sponsors rarely grant such permission.

The strict Saudi Arabian courts continue to impose corporal punishment, including amputations of hands and feet for robbery and floggings for drunkenness. Capital punishment is common. Saudi officials conduct beheadings in public squares on Friday, just after the noon prayers, and all are welcome to attend.

I was visiting a client in Riyadh, the Saudi capital, on one occasion, and he asked me to join him for a car ride into the old city to show me something. Grinning, he placed his hand on my back and led me out to his car. I asked what he wanted to show me, and he calmly said that we were going to visit a place called "Chop-Chop Square." It did not sound like a particularly Arabic name, but I put that to the back of my mind as we drove. As the streets became narrower and congested with foot traffic, the car was parked, and we walked with the throng in the direction of the square. We came close to an area called Deerah, in the heart of old Riyadh near the souk. I recognized it from my last visit and recalled scenes of old Arab men smoking hookahs and drinking tea, the smell of sweet aromatic spices and incense, and the call of hawkers selling Persian carpets.

We entered the square and I saw several hundred people jostling for position facing a platform. Locals looked over their shoulders and saw me, then smiled and moved aside as I made my way, guided by my host, toward the front of the square. I had started to realize what my companion wanted to show me, but, by this point, I could not think of any way to back out. I looked at my colleague. He beamed a smile and nodded at me to keep walking. My stomach turned.

We stopped about five rows from the front. I saw the chopping block, confirming my worst fears. A policeman smiled at me, obviously proud that I was to witness the superior form of Islamic justice.

Jailers led a hooded man onto the platform. A swordsman followed behind. Many people cheered. A small section was screaming at the prisoner. My host leaned in and motioned toward that group. "Those are the family of the man this criminal killed," he said in a hushed voice.

I gestured toward the prisoner. "He's a murderer?"

My host nodded.

A few other men gathered around the convict. One gave him what looked like an injection of some sort. "A sedative," said my host.

I gulped and began sweating profusely. The hooded convict knelt and the swordsman raised his gleaming steel blade. I planned to look away when the final moment came, but, before I could, the blade fell swiftly. With a whack, the murderer's head fell to the platform, while his body slumped on the other side of the block. A pool of blood covered a large part of the platform, and I felt extremely uneasy.

The crowd cheered and chanted "Allahu Akbar" (God is great).

My host asked if I wanted to stay to see the next criminal to meet his fate. I declined and, without waiting for him, made my way back toward the car. Several locals snickered at my uneasiness and at what was probably my extremely pale complexion as I forged my way past the crowd.

I later learned that prisoners often receive no official warning of the imminence of their execution. Their first realization of what is about to happen to them is when their jailers shackle them and bring them into Chop-Chop Square. I also learned that execution-ers typically shoot women, instead of beheading them.

For the Saudi people, these customs go back hundreds of years. The essence of "old Arabia" can still be found not only in their approach to corporal punishment, but in regional commerce as well. I observed fascinating action as it has been conducted for centuries along the busy side streets and the Dubai Creek in a section called Deira Dubai. Each evening, numerous long, flat, wooden sailing vessels called dhows are docked three and four deep along the creek. Antiquated canvas-covered diesel trucks line up, stretching several blocks to deliver their cargo of just about every imaginable prod-uct. Small livestock, jewelry, clothing, trinkets, and housewares are all manifested to these boats. As the process unfolds, thousands of boxes and crates are stacked several feet high along the promenade, as frenzied laborers load them onto the dhows for their voyage.

This scene of utter mayhem goes late into the night. The next morning, you would think that the previous night was all a dream. Astonishingly, during your morning walk, you see the Deira Dubai area totally deserted. By this time, the dhows are already a few hours into their journeys to Iran, the Gulf, Africa, India, and Pakistan.

A short distance away is the Gold Souk, known locally as the City of Gold. In a maze of narrow streets and partly covered alleyways are countless shop windows, brightly lit and filled with twenty-two- and twenty-four-karat gold bangles, necklaces, ear-rings, bracelets and brooches that are sold by weight. People from all over the world wander these streets looking for bargains to take back home. Unimaginable amounts of gold fill the showcases in the store windows as ladies gaze at beautiful jewelry and men admire expensive watches. Deals can be found here, but typically only after spending a few hours haggling. Approximately seven hundred tons of gold jewelry is purchased here each year.

You can see conservative Moslem women wearing *abayas* (long black cloaks) and covering their faces with *boshiyas* (black veils) at many of the counters. For them, this is no casual shopping trip. It is, in fact, a kind of insurance to protect themselves financially from "Triple *Talaq*," a Sunni Islamic tenet that allows a husband to divorce his wife by saying to her "*talaq, talaq, talaq*" ("I divorce you, I divorce you, I divorce you"). No fault needs to be found with the wife for a divorce to take place, other than that she "displeases" her husband. She must then leave the husband's home. The husband is not financially responsible for supporting his divorced wife, nor does the wife have a right to any portion of their combined assets.

In most Islamic states, it is unacceptable for a divorced woman to live alone, so she has no choice but to return with virtually nothing to live with her parents or other close relatives. Obviously, she is better off financially if she has a few pounds of gold concealed beneath her flowing robes.

I share these anecdotes not to repulse you, but to give you a perspective on why long-held customs often cannot be reconciled to today's sensitivities. Even Conscientious Equity will not quickly overcome long- and fast-held beliefs.

## THIRTEEN CENTURIES OF HERMITAGE

Our perceptions of Korea, like Japan, are colored by war. Yet the success of South Korea is something that should make Americans very proud.

Korea has a history of more than thirteen hundred years as a distinct nation. It was unified for the first time in the seventh century under the Silla Kingdom. The subsequent stability and centralized administration allowed the rise of a national consciousness. The Silla Kingdom began to decline in the ninth century and gave way to the Goryeo dynasty, which was founded in 936 and lasted until 1392. It is from the Goryeo period that we get the anglicized name of Korea.

Because the Goryeo monarchs were closely allied with the declining Yuan (Mongol) dynasty in China, a rival general was able to gain support from the incoming Ming dynasty to oust the last Goryeo ruler. In 1392, the Choson dynasty (the name means morning freshness or morning calm) was founded and established its new capital in Hanyang, later known as Seoul.

During the Choson dynasty, from 1392 to 1910, the outside world referred to Korea as the "hermit kingdom." The Silla, Goryeo, and Choson dynasties were all known for their stern isolationist policies and hyper-xenophobia. They considered all Westerners barbarians and did not allow Westerners to land on their shores. The kingdom's people lived in total seclusion and traded very little with foreign lands. Virtually all their trade was with China, and, under all three dynasties, Korea was a Chinese protectorate. China has historically viewed the Korean peninsula as a buffer zone against Japan and, therefore, has been engaged in Korean politics for centuries.

The United States and Korea signed the Treaty of Chemulpo (an old name for Inchon) in May 1882. Korea's first covenant with a Western country was agreed to grudgingly, as Korea was under pressure from American "gunboat diplomacy." The treaty allowed the United States to establish an embassy and granted trade relations. It also guaranteed the safety of missionaries, who soon arrived to set up churches, medical clinics, schools, and universities. Yonsei University, today one of the most respected private institutions in Korea, was founded by an American missionary.

During Japan's colonial rule (1910–1945) over Korea, the Japanese worked feverishly to abolish all traces of independent Korean identity. The Japanese made worship at Shinto shrines compulsory, radically modified school curricula, and forbade schools from teaching or using the Korean language. Newspapers could not publish in Korean. Universities could not teach Korean history, and Korean textbooks were burned. The Japanese used Korea as a base to produce raw materials and industrial products for Japan's expansion into China and as a source of food for the Japanese homeland. This period was marked, as well, by the sad story of the "comfort women." As many as three hundred thousand Korean women were kidnapped from their villages and enslaved to provide sexual services for Japanese military personnel throughout Asia.

Koreans still have very bitter memories of this period, and these memories are always ready to explode. During one of my recent visits to Seoul, I noticed no demonstrators in front of the U.S. embassy, which allowed me to breeze in for a meeting. It turned out that all of the demonstrators were around the corner at the Japanese embassy decrying the Japanese prime minister's recent visit to a World War II military personnel gravesite.

The Allies liberated the Korean peninsula from Japanese colonial rule in August 1945, close to the end of World War II. Suddenly, more Americans were entering Korea than ever before—not only missionaries and entrepreneurs, as in the past, but also thousands of troops connected with the American Military Government, which had assumed the administrative and police duties of the defeated Japanese. These troops acted as the country's caretakers until Koreans could elect a government for the first time in their history. The election was delayed for three years because of the inexperience of Korea's politicians and the partition between the north and south at the thirty-eighth parallel. Initially intended as a temporary measure to facilitate the surrender of Japanese troops in both the American and Soviet zones, the partition soon became the cause of political and military confrontation.

In 1945, the Soviets had hurriedly established a Communist regime in the north, and they later refused to agree on arrangements for nationwide elections to unify the country. In 1948, after holding its own elections under UN supervision, the south set up a democratic form of government to replace the American Military Government. South Korea was henceforth known as the Republic of Korea (ROK). Simultaneously, the North Koreans proclaimed a separate Communist state, to be known as the Democratic People's Republic of Korea (DPRK), under the control of the Soviet Union, with Kim Il Sung as its leader.

In 1948, after the elections in the south, the United States announced the pending withdrawal of all U.S. troops (with the exception of some advisors) and publicly proclaimed a Pacific defense rim that excluded South Korea. At the time, the ROK was underdeveloped and mostly agrarian, and the Korean peninsula's industry and natural resources were heavily concentrated in the north. Meanwhile, with the assistance of the Soviet Union, North Korea quickly armed itself to the teeth.

The almost total withdrawal of U.S. forces from South Korea by the middle of 1949 left the south defended by a weak and inexperienced ROK army. On June 25, 1950, the DPRK launched a massive surprise attack, quickly capturing Seoul and pushing the ROK and limited American forces to a small perimeter around the southern port city of Pusan. Just when it appeared that South Korea was lost and the ROK and American forces would be pushed into the Sea of Japan, one of the most ingenious military operations of the twentieth century unfolded. On September 15, 1950, under the command of General Douglas MacArthur, the United States launched an amphibious landing at Inchon, a feat that many had considered impossible. The North Koreans fighting in South Korea were cut off and began a haphazard retreat. In just a few months, U.S. troops captured Pyongyang and reached the Yalu River border with China. Kim Il Sung and his government were forced to take refuge in China.

Then, one million Communist Chinese troops came pouring over the border.

The combatants fought to a stalemate. In July 1953, the United States, China, and North Korea signed an armistice ending the hostilities. The agreement established a two-and-a-half-mile wide, one hundred and fifty–mile long demilitarized zone along the thirty-eighth parallel. The number of American servicemen and women who lost their lives in the Korean War totaled 54,246. To this day, South Korea has not signed the armistice, and the two nations are still technically at war.

There is no starker contrast between evil and good in the world today than that of the hermit gulag of North Korea and the incredible economic success of South Korea—a success paid for in blood and treasure by the United States. South Korea's success is due in large part to the generosity and sacrifice of the American people, which should make all of us very proud. The enactment of the pending trade agreement between our two great nations should be a reason for celebration and a crowning moment in our shared history.

During my numerous visits to the Land of Morning Calm, I have met many of our servicemen and women whose dedication has allowed South Korea to become the world's eleventh largest economy—an incredible accomplishment for a country about the size of Minnesota, with virtually no natural resources. During my first visit to Seoul in the late seventies, however, I was struck by how poor and underdeveloped the country was. The winter was biting cold. Hillsides were bare, as people scavenged firewood to provide fleeting moments of warmth. Sprawling villages, with their distinctive undulating ceramic roofs and wooden plank doors opening to small alleyways, gave little relief from the elements.

Women, their glowing red faces always quick to offer a smile, bundled themselves up with everything they owned and shopped early each morning for their daily meals at outdoor markets. Butchers feverishly sawed freshly slaughtered carcasses that released condensation into the cold, brisk air from the body heat still trapped in the animals' flesh. Fish vendors gutted strange-looking creatures from the surrounding seas. Large stockpots boiled entrails of cows, goats, and dogs (the smell, for a non-connoisseur, was unbearable). Military checkpoints, manned by heavily armed soldiers, appeared randomly. The eerie wail of air-raid sirens during all hours signaled one drill after another that brought everything to a grinding halt. Just thirty miles from Seoul's northern gate, the brainwashed million-man army of North Korea was in a continuous state of high alert. Tank traps meant to slow down the omnipresent risk of a North Korean blitzkrieg dotted the landscape. At every turn, there were reminders that all hell could break loose at any moment.

To witness South Korea transform itself, seemingly overnight, during the lead-up to the 1988 Olympics was fascinating. Seoul shrugged off its backwater mentality of being under military siege and morphed into a glamorous city of glass towers, expansive parks, and high fashion. The towering buildings of Yoido and Gangnam-ku, the Olympic Village, the promenade and the beautiful bridges along the Han River are truly remarkable. Even the rowdy and raunchy hot spots of Itaewon—once a soldier's paradise of well-deserved R&R at the center of Seoul—have been reinvented into a respectable enclave of nightclubs, restaurants, and shopping complexes.

South Korea has come so far. The checkpoints and air raid drills are a distant memory. The high-profile presence of the U.S. military in and around Seoul has vanished. It has been a remarkable act of reinvention after a seemingly endless period of isolation.

If you believe in the sacrifice brave Americans made so that fifty million South Koreans could live in freedom, if you respect the devotion to duty of our military that has guaranteed that freedom over the past sixty years, then it would be the worst kind of hypocrisy to play politics with their sacrifice and deny freedom of trade between the United States and South Korea, which is precisely what our Congress is doing by not ratifying the United States-Republic of Korea (KORUS) Free Trade Agreement.

## THE LEGACY OF VIETNAM

The Vietnam War was a painful experience for American soldiers. Those who followed orders and pulled their triggers may have escaped North Vietnamese bullets and booby traps, but not the psychological ambush that their fellow citizens inflicted on their scarred souls stateside. There was no parade for the soldiers returning home, no heroes' welcome or even a thank you. For many returning from Vietnam, home no longer felt like home. Some veterans of the war returned to various countries in Asia and found themselves more at home there. Many have become valuable assets for both the United States and their adoptive countries in forming knowledgeable cultural and business links between the two as the Asian economies moved toward the millennium. I have had the privilege to know a number of American soldiers who, after completing their tours in Vietnam, felt disillusioned and settled in the Philippines, Indonesia, and Thailand. Many still serve our nation by representing American manufacturers in their adopted countries. They have been indispensable in generating billions of dollars of American exports.

Ed Turner was one of these courageous Vietnam veterans. Known to his friends as E.T., he was a heavyweight club fighter who became a gunner on a gunship called Spooky. Military duty on a gunship—a slow, low-flying aircraft with little armor—was extremely dangerous.

At the time of his service, the United States was carrying out a massive herbicidal program, which ran from 1961 through 1971. The aim of the program was twofold: to destroy the cover provided by the thick forest and to deny food to the enemy. The U.S. Department of Veterans Affairs has listed prostate cancer, respiratory cancer, multiple myeloma, type II diabetes, Hodgkin's disease, lymphoma, soft tissue sarcoma, chloracne (a skin disorder), and peripheral neuropathy (a nerve disorder) as side effects of Agent Orange, the mixture of herbicide used in the program. During his tour of duty, Ed was exposed to this dangerous compound.

After his honorable discharge, Ed used his G.I. Bill benefits to earn an engineering degree from the University of Maryland. He then returned to Asia in self-imposed exile, never again to live in the United States.

After I hired Ed to run the engineering department of my company in Manila, we traveled together to Vietnam in 1991. It was just sixteen years after the fall of Saigon and the final American military and civilian departures. It was Ed's first time back. Having been too young for the wartime draft, I was setting foot in Vietnam for the first time.

Before the U.S. embargo was lifted in 1994, Vietnam was expected to become the next Asian tiger. Many believed that it would attract massive foreign investment, especially from the United States, with thousands of Americans rushing to visit the storied land. The anticipated planeloads of tourists and business people would need hotels and resorts. With this in mind, the senior management of Saigon Tourist, a state-owned Vietnamese company with exclusive rights to many sectors of Vietnam's tourist and transportation industry, made a trip to the Philippines to study its tourist infrastructure. At the top of the managers' to-do list in the Philippines was finding a company to set up manufacturing in Saigon to create products for the new hospitality industry. The

Philippine government arranged for the group to tour our factory in Manila.

At the invitation of the managing director of Saigon Tourist, Ed and I found ourselves on a plane to Saigon. As the wheels touched down, I could see Ed churn uncomfortably in his seat. He was dreadfully worried that the Vietnamese government would somehow be aware of his role in the war and whisk him away, never to be seen again. He trembled as he handed the immigration officer his passport. It was an incredible relief when we cleared customs and found our driver awaiting us. These were clearly going to be an emotional few days.

The person sitting across the table from us during negotiations over a deal for our services had been a colonel in the North Vietnamese Army during the war. With the embargo still in effect, we were the first Americans he ever received. Sixteen years before our meeting, he had been killing Americans. On my side of the table, we had Spooky's gunner, who had taken an untold number of Vietnamese lives. It was a remarkable situation.

During a break in our negotiations, Ed and I had our driver take us to the U.S. embassy compound. It was eerily overgrown. The windows were missing, and lush tropical flora grew into and out of the building, as though it were some long-abandoned castle. We gazed across the courtyard, where the Tet Offensive had raged for several hours in 1968. We looked up to the roof, where the lucky few had boarded the last chopper out on April 30, 1975, during operation Frequent Wind. I found myself transfixed.

The next thing I remember is being shoved into the car by our nervous driver, who was terrified that he would be arrested or that an angry mob might form, imperiling all of us. As we sped away, I looked at Ed, whom I had always considered a man of steel. The tough guy had lost his composure and tears were streaming down his face, as the sight of the dilapidated U.S. embassy rekindled memories that Ed had tried to suppress. We returned to the negotiating table, but "negotiation" was a euphemism. The terms offered by the colonel to set up a factory in Saigon constituted one of the most lopsided, ridiculous deals I had ever come across. The government's thinking at the time was that foreign investors would pay anything to queue up for the Vietnam gold rush—a rush that never happened. It took the deaths of China's Mao Tse-tung and his revolutionary comrades before China could boom. In the same way, the North Vietnamese and Viet Cong military elite that still run Vietnam—now mostly octogenarians—will have to pass on before this beautiful country can break the shackles that keep it from fulfilling its potential. Ed and I walked away from the proffered deal, and I have never regretted it.

Not long ago, I spoke to E.T. for the last time. He was lying in bed at his home in Santa Rosa, Laguna, about forty miles south of Manila. His wife had called me, frantic for assistance persuading him to go to the hospital, because he was very sick. E.T. came to the phone and said, in his distinctive growl, "Don't listen to her. I am doing just fine." He took his final breath an hour later. I don't know if it was the last thirty years of hard living, the Agent Orange, or his self-imposed exile that finally got him.

I do know this: Ed was fighting for America until the day he died. His design and engineering work over the past thirty years produced overseas contracts worth tens of millions of dollars for American exporters, creating thousands of good-paying jobs for American workers. When we last spoke, this giant man with an ego as big as Texas, the toughness of a cornered grizzly bear, and a heart of pure gold had one last request: to die peacefully at home in his adoptive country.

## How I Nearly Became a Chieftain's Son-in-Law

I was a music student on an exchange program in London during college when I befriended a Nigerian student named Eugene

Chidi. Just before I began my senior year back in the States, Eugene told me that his family needed someone to make contacts and run errands in the United States for the family's group of companies, based in Lagos. He thought I would be a good person for the job.

I wasn't entirely sure how doing such work matched my ambitions at the time, but the notion piqued my interest. From the time I was a child, I would stare for long stretches at the maps in the *National Geographic* magazines stacked in my family's small living room, trying to memorize the geography of places outside America. I imagined faraway lands and envisioned what it would be like to visit these exotic locales and meet the people who lived there. Memories of my map-gazing days and the idea of working with people half a globe away intrigued me. I told Eugene that I would be willing to take on the work, and he recommended me to his uncle in Lagos.

A few weeks passed. I didn't hear anything more from Eugene, and I all but forgot about the conversation. Then, the phone rang with my first assignment. Just like that, I had stepped into the world of international entrepreneurship.

Nigeria is a major exporter of crude oil and an important member of OPEC. Its crude, known as "bonny light," is of the highest quality and always in high demand. The family for which I was now working was politically powerful and active in the oil business, among other enterprises. The head of the clan was a well-respected and engaging Nigerian chief.

The Nigerians wanted to help blacks in America. One of their strategies was to offer crude oil to high-profile African-American politicians at subsidized rates to show their support. I arranged and sat through some of the meetings connected with these transactions, including one with the borough president of Manhattan, who also owned the largest black radio station in New York City. You can imagine the surprise on the faces of those who attended the meeting when a young white boy came walking in with the Nigerian chief's entourage to discuss oil deals. I attended similar meetings with well-known African American members of Congress, as well, and, I'm sure, generated similar confusion.

Some time after these meetings, the chief invited me to spend three weeks in Nigeria as part of my training. He told me that, during my visit, we would attend the coronation of the *oba* (king) of one of the Yoruba regions. This thrilled me; for the first time, my fanciful images of remote places would come to life. I found many elements of the trip unforgettable. At one meeting with government bureaucrats, our people put a briefcase full of *naira* (the Nigerian currency) on the conference table in exchange for some business favor. I was amazed at how casually the officials accepted it but soon came to understand that business transactions took place differently there.

I also vividly recall our daily drives to downtown Lagos. The chief lived in a walled compound in a beautiful and prosperous suburb. Outside the walls, conditions were emphatically different. For two days, we passed a dead person lying on the side of the road, his decomposing body sending off a gag-inducing stench that called to flies from all corners of the neighborhood. Imagine the impact such a body would have if it spent two minutes on an American street. Here, though, people walked around the corpse, barely noticing.

What I remember most from the trip is the coronation day of the oba. I dressed in traditional Nigerian formal attire. I wore an *agbada* (a long flowing robe) with matching *sokoto* (loose, baggy pants), and I had strands of beads around my neck made from coral and bones. I sat on the stage during the ceremony and did my best to look as if I belonged there.

After the coronation, there was a procession in the streets, and I marched alongside the chief. There were loud drums beating and crowds of people dancing and chanting hysterically all around us. The chief carried wads of *naira* and peeled off bills to give away to the celebrants. At one point, though I didn't notice it, a local thief reached into the chief's *agbada* and took a fistful of his *naira*.

Early that evening, with many local dignitaries at the chief's compound still celebrating with music, dancing, and food, there was a loud commotion at the front gate. A rowdy gang of shouting, gesturing men dragged the limp, bloodied body of some poor, barely alive soul to the middle of the courtyard. The music stopped and everyone turned their eyes to this raggedy group of vigilantes and their prisoner. One of the men announced that they had captured the thief who had stolen the chief's money. The chief did not take long to decide the pickpocket's fate: death by stoning.

The vigilantes formed a circle around the thief and proceeded to carry out the sentence. The wailing of the condemned man and the thuds of stones breaking his bones assaulted my ears and made me shiver. I had experienced many reminders on this trip that I was far from home, but nothing as pronounced or as indelible as this. I stood with others on a balcony and watched, stunned, trying to reconcile this spectacle with everything I believed about justice. Again, I share this story as a glimpse into an accepted Nigerian notion of justice at the time, not to disparage the country.

Amazingly, the revelry resumed soon thereafter, though I was still so flustered that I couldn't have partied if someone had held a gun to my head and demanded I do so. To regain my equilibrium, I took a walk with the chief's daughter. She had been studying medicine in Cairo and she was stunning, especially now in her bright blue *kaba* (a one-piece dress) that wrapped around her and her matching *gele* (headpiece). We had become well acquainted during my stay at the chief's compound, and I was extremely attracted to her.

We strolled through the village holding hands. The horrors of the stoning passed, replaced by the strong sense of satisfaction that came from being with this woman. That did not last long, though.

When we were well outside the compound, she stopped and turned to me, saying, "When are you going to tell the chief about us?"

The question startled me and started my heart pounding all over again. It took me a long moment to recover. I was finally able to choke out, "What exactly should I be telling the chief?" She quickly responded that she would be graduating from medical school in four months and that she would be ready to join me in the United States after that. She went on to add that she knew the chief was fond of me and that she was sure he would approve of our marriage—our marriage!—once he got over the initial shock of learning that we were together in that way.

Not only was I not thinking about marriage at all at that stage in my life, but I also was not so certain that the chief would take the idea of my marrying his daughter so well. I had just seen this man condemn someone to immediate death. I could imagine him reacting equally aggressively to the discovery that his favorite child and I were secretly making lifetime commitments while I was a guest under his roof. I gathered my wits as rapidly as I could and told this beautiful woman, whom I was nowhere near ready to marry, that I thought it would be a bad time to burden her father with something like this. He had numerous business deals pending and quite a bit to consider. Instead, I would find the right moment to broach the subject during his upcoming visit to New York.

Fortunately, this approach was enough for her at that moment. I was happy about that because, although I did not want to marry her, I also did not want to break her heart. When we walked back into the compound, both of us were smiling, although anyone who looked closely could have seen the sweat that still sprouted on my brow.

Shortly after my return to the United States, there was a military coup in Nigeria. My friends fell out of favor. Neither the chief nor his daughter ever showed up in New York, and my work evaporated.

I never got the chance to become Nigerian royalty, but I was left with the indelible impression of a world completely different from any I had ever known before.

This was the beginning for me. This experience—the strangeness, the exposure to a culture so unlike mine, the fascinating people, and even the starkly different ways of solving problems—kindled a passion in me that no one could ever extinguish. A passion that ultimately led me to my vision of Conscientious Equity.

It seems appropriate here to leave you with my beginnings, because I hope this book has inspired a sense of new beginnings in you.

# NOTES

## TWO  A SHIP THAT SAILED LONG AGO

1. "A Century of Lawmaking for a New Nation: U.S. Congressional Documents and Debates, 1774–1875." *American Memory*. Library of Congress, n.d. Web. 22 Apr 2010. <http://memory.loc.gov/cgi-bin/ampage?collId=llsl&fileName=001/llsl001.db&recNum=147>.
2. Charles Henry Butler, *The Treaty Making Power of the United States*. Banks Law Publishing Co., 1902. Print.
3. Alexander Hamilton. *Report on Manufactures*. Washington, D.C.: Government Printing Office. 2009. Print.
4. Thomas Jefferson. *Notes on the State of Virginia*. Richmond, VA: J.W. Randolph, 1853. Print.
5. "Tariff of Abominations." *NationMaster*. N.p., n.d. Web. 22 Apr 2010. <http://www.nationmaster.com/encyclopedia/Tariff-of-Abominations>.
6. Charles Adams. *When in the Course of Human Events*. Lanham, MD: Rowman & Littlefield, 2005. Print.

7. "Smoot-Hawley Tariff." *EH.net*. Economic History Services, n.d. Web. 22 Apr 2010. <http://eh.net/encyclopedia/article/obrien.hawley-smoot.tariff>.

8 Milton Friedman. *Capitalism and Freedom*, Chicago, IL: University of Chicago Press, 2002. Print.

## THREE   TAKING BACK THE KEYS TO THE BUS

1. Anup Shah. "WTO Protests in Seattle, 1999." *Global Issues*. N.p., 18 02 2001. Web. 22 Apr 2010. <http://www.globalissues.org/article/46/wto-protests-in-seattle-1999>.

2. Douglas A. Irwin. "GATT Turns 60." *Free Trade.org*. The Cato Institute, 09 04 2007. Web. 22 Apr 2010. <http://www.freetrade.org/node/608>.

3. Reem Heakal. "What Is The World Trade Organization?" *Investopedia. com*. Investopedia ULC, n.d. Web. 22 Apr 2010. <http://www.investo-pedia.com/articles/03/040203.asp>

4. "Top Reasons to Oppose the WTO." *Global Exchange.org*. Global Exchange, 09 09 2008. Web. 22 Apr 2010. <http://www.globalexchange. org/campaigns/wto/OpposeWTO.html>

5. Sallie James. "U.S. Response to Gambling Dispute Reveals Weak Hand." *Free Trade Bulletin*. 24 (2006): Print.

6. "Antigua wins Internet gambling fight against US." *Out-Law.com*. Pinsent Masons LLP, 05 04 2004. Web. 22 Apr 2010. <http://www.out-law.com/page-4504>.

7. Wayne M. Morrison, Wayne M. Section 301 of the Trade Act of 1974 Its Operation and Issues Involving Its Use by the United States. [Washington, D.C.]: Congressional Research Service, Library of Congress, 1999. Print.

8. "The trade talks that never conclude." *Economist* 31 07 2008. Print.

9. "Doha Development Round." *Wikipedia*. Web. <http://en.wikipedia.org/wiki/Doha_Development_Round>

## FOUR   PLAYING BY THE RULES WHEN THE RULES DON'T EXIST

1. Michael Johnston. "Corruption and Poverty." *Forbes* 22 01 2009. Print.

2. "Secretary-General's message at the opening of the High-level Political Conference for the Purpose of Signing the UN Convention against

Corruption [delivered by Hans Corell, Under-Secretary-General for Legal Affairs]." *UN.org.* United Nations, 09 12 2003. Web. 22 Apr 2010. <http://www.un.org/apps/sg/sgstats.asp?nid=685>.

3. "CPI 2008 Table." *Transparency.org.* Transparency International, n.d. Web. 22 Apr 2010. <http://www.transparency.org/news_room/in_focus/2008/cpi2008/cpi_2008_table>.

4. *The World Factbook.* CIA, n.d. Web. 22 Apr 2010. <https://www.cia.gov/library/publications/the-world-factbook/rankorder/2004rank.html?countryCode=&rankAnchorRow=#>.

5. Abdul Khalik. "Supreme Court Reform in Danger: Experts." *The Jakarta Post* 24 09 2008. Print.

6. "We Practically Own Everything in the Philippines: Imelda | Reyna Elena Dot Com." Reyna Elena. Web. 02 July 2010. <http://reynaelena.com/2007/07/31/amin-to-yan-pa-at-yun-pa/>.

7. "Advice to JDV: Cut and Cut Cleanly—INQUIRER.net, Philippine News for Filipinos." Opinion—INQUIRER.net. Web. 02 July 2010. <http://opinion.inquirer.net/inquireropinion/columns/view/20080204–116578/Advice-to-JDV-Cut-and-cut-cleanly>.

8. "Foreign Corrupt Practices Act's Antibribery Provisions." The 'Lectric Law Library's Entrance & Welcome. Web. 02 July 2010. <http://www.lectlaw.com/files/bur21.htm>.

9. "OECD Convention on Combating Bribery of Foreign Public Officials in International Business Transactions." *OECD.org.* Organisation for Economic Co-operation and Development, n.d. Web. 22 Apr 2010. <http://www.oecd.org/document/21/0,3343,en_2649_34859_2017813_1_1_1_1,00.html>.

## FIVE   INGENUITY IS NOT A
## PUBLIC SERVICE

1. Paul Sweeting. "Copyright industries growing part of GDP." *Video Business.com.* N.p., 30 01 2007. Web. <http://www.videobusiness.com/article/CA6411741.html>.

2. Stephen E. Siwek. "Copyright Industries in the U.S. Economy: The 2006 Report." *Economists Incorporated for the International Intellectual Property Alliance.* Print.

3. Gloria Gonzalez. "Top risk in China? Intellectual property theft." *Financial Week* 13 08 2007. Print.

4. "U.S. Trade with China." U.S. Government Printing Office Home Page. Web. 02 July 2010. <http://www.gpo.gov/fdsys/pkg/CHRG-110hhrg11040304/html/CHRG-110hhrg11040304.htm>.

5. Kevin Maney. "If pirating grows, it may not be the end of music world." *USA Today* 03 05 2005. Print.

6. "China produces 500m pirated books a year." *Bookseller.com* 19 03 2007: n. pag. Web. <http://www.thebookseller.com/news/35825-china-produces-500m-pirated-books-a-year.html>.

7. Ted C. Fishman. "How to Stop Intellectual Property Theft in China." *Inc.* 01 06 2006. Print.

8. "What is CCC Mark?." *CCC-Mark.com*. N.p., n.d. Web. <http://www.ccc-mark.com/what-is-ccc-mark.html>.

9. Gonzalez, Gloria. "China: Risks & Rewards | Business Insurance." Business Insurance News, Analysis & Articles. Web. 02 July 2010. <http://www.businessinsurance.com/article2000483>.

10. Corey Boles. "U.S. Says China, Russia Lag On Intellectual-Property Crime." *Wall Street Journal* 26 04 2008. Print.

11. "Intellectual Property: Source of innovation, creativity, growth and progress." *iccwbo.org*. International Chamber of Commerce, 01 08 2005. Web. <www.iccwbo.org/uploadedFiles/ICC/policy/intellectual_property/Statements/BASCAP_IP_pub.pdf>.

12 "Counterfeit Fighters | Packaging Online." Packaging Online |. Web. 02 July 2010. <http://www.packaging-online.com/paperboard-packaging-content/counterfeit-fighters>.

13. "Statement Of Jon W. Dudas Acting Under Secretary Of Commerce For Intellectual Property And Acting Director Of The United States Patent And Trademark Office Before The Committee On Judiciary United States Senate March 23, 2004." *United States Department of Commerce Office of General Counsel*. United States Department of Commerce, n.d. Web. <http://www.ogc.doc.gov/ogc/legreg/testimon/108s/dudas0323.htm>

## SIX  THE KIND OF FARM AID WILLIE NELSON NEVER IMAGINED

1. Chris Edwards. "Agricultural Subsidies." *downsizinggovernment.org*. The Cato Institute, June 1, 2009. Web. <http://www.downsizinggovernment.org/agriculture/subsidies>.

2. Ibid.
3. Dan Morgan, Gilbert M. Gaul, and Sarah Cohen. "Farm Program Pays $1.3 Billion to People Who Don't Farm." *Washington Post* 06 07 2006, Print.
4. "Agricultural Subsidies." Downsizing the Federal Government. Web. July 5, 2010. <http://www.downsizinggovernment.org/agriculture/subsidies>.
5. Daniel Griswold, Stephen Slivinski, and Christopher Preble. "Six Reasons to Kill Farm Subsidies and Trade Barriers: A no-nonsense reform strategy." *Reason Magazine* February 2, 2006. Print.
6 Ibid.
7. "Agricultural Trade Liberalization." Washington, D.C.: Congressional Budget Office, 2006. Print.

## SEVEN   SANCTION FEVER

1. Jona Lendering. "Megarian Decree." N.p., *Livius.org* 31 03 2006: Web. <http://www.livius.org/mea-mem/megara/decree.html>.
2. Bruce Bartlett. "What's Wrong With Trade Sanctions." *Cato.org*. The Cato Institute, n.d. Web. <http://www.cato.org/pubs/pas/pa064.html>.
3. "The Panay Incident." *Onwar.com*. N.p., December 16, 2000. Web. <http://www.onwar.com/aced/data/juliet/japanus1937.htm http://www.cato.org/pubs/pas/pa064.html>.
4. Gary Clyde Hufbauer, Kimberly Ann Elliott, Tess Cyrus, and Elizabeth Winston. "US Economic Sanctions: Their Impact on Trade, Jobs, and Wages." *iie.com*. The Peterson Institute for International Economics, April 1, 1997. Web. <http://www.iie.com/publications/wp/wp.cfm?ResearchID=149>.
5. *http://www.cato.org/*. The Cato Institute, n.d. Web.

## EIGHT   A LITTLE KNOWLEDGE MAKES A DANGEROUS LEADER

1. M. Angeles Villarreal. "U.S.-Colombia Trade Promotion Agreement." *CRS Report for Congress*. Washington, D.C.: The Library of Congress, 2006. Print.

2. "China Fears Bond Crisis as It Slams Quantitative Easing—Telegraph." Telegraph.co.uk: News, Business, Sport, the Daily Telegraph Newspaper, Sunday Telegraph—Telegraph. Web. July 5, 2010. <http://www.tele-graph.co.uk/finance/newsbysector/banksandfinance/5286832/China-fears-bond-crisis-as-it-slams-quantitative-easing.html>.

3. "FRB: H.6 Release—Discontinuance of M3." Board of Governors of the Federal Reserve System. Web. July 5, 2010. <http://www.federalreserve.gov/releases/h6/discm3.htm>.

4. "Miller to Uribe: Colombia Must Improve Investigations and Prosecutions of Labor Killings." Committee on Education and Labor, n.d. Web. April 22, 2010. <http://www.house.gov/apps/list/speech/edla-bor_dem/091508Uribe.html>.

5. "Free Trade, Free Markets: Rating the Congress." *Free Trade.org.* The Cato Institute, n.d. Web. <http://www.cato.org/trade-immigration/congress/?>.

6. "Testimony of Thea Mei Lee Policy Director American Federation of Labor and Congress of Industrial Organizations (AFL-CIO) Before the Senate Finance Committee 'U.S.-Panama Trade Promotion Agreement.'" N.p., n.d. Web. <http://finance.senate.gov/hearings/testimony/2009test/052109tltest.pdf.>. "Fast Facts on AFL-CIO Convention & Membership." *aflcio.org.* N.p., n.d. Web. <http://www.aflcio.org/aboutus/thisistheaflcio/convention/2005/upload/fastfacts.pdf.>.

## NINE  OUR MOST VALUABLE IMPORTS

1. "Omid Kordestani's Commencement Address at SJSU." youtube.com. Web. <http://www.youtube.com/watch?v=HJer30-Lj2s>.

2. "Immigrant Backgrounder." Migration Policy Institute. October 2006. Washington, D.C.

3. Jonathan Bowles and Tara Colton. "A World of Opportunity." New York, NY: The Center for an Urban Future, 2007. Print.

4. Cokie Roberts and Steven V. Roberts. "Help Wanted: Successful Immigrants to Save U.S." New York, NY. Newspaper Enterprise Association, 2010. Print.

5. "Comprehensive Immigration Reform for America's Security and Prosperity." *reformimmigrationforamerica.org.* Web. <http://reformimmigrationforamerica.org/blog/summary-of-representative-gutierrezs-cir-asap-act/>.

## TEN  THAT'S WHY THEY CALL HIM
## "CHIEF EXECUTIVE"

1. Susan Ariel Aaronson. "Who Decides? Congress and the Debate Over Trade Policy in 1934 and 1974." *cfr.org.* Council on Foreign Relations, November 11, 1999. Web. <http://www.cfr.org/publication/8707/who_decides_congress_and_the_debate_over_trade_policy_in_1934_and_1974.html?excerpt=1>.

2. Aaronson, Susan A. Taking Trade to the Streets: the Lost History of Public Efforts to Shape Globalization. Ann Arbor: Univ. of Michigan, 2001. Print.

3. "Reciprocal Trade Agreement." Encyclopedia of American History. Answers Corporation, 2006. *Answers.com.* Web. <http://www.answers.com/topic/reciprocal-trade-agreement>.

4. Fred C. Bergsten. "The Democrats' Dangerous Trade Games." *Wall Street Journal,* May 20, 2008, Print.

5. Lee Hudson Teslik. "Fast-Track Trade Promotion Authority and Its Impact on U.S. Trade Policy." *cfr.org.* Council on Foreign Relations, June 25, 2007. Web. <http://www.cfr.org/publication/13663/>.

6. Lenore Sek. "Trade Promotion Authority (Fast-Track Authority for Trade Agreements): Background and Developments in the 107th Congress." *Issue Brief for Congress.* Washington, D.C.: The Library of Congress, 2003. Print.

7. "About the Bretton Woods Committee." *brettonwoods.org.* The Bretton Woods Committee, n.d. Web. <http://www.brettonwoods.org/index.php/167/About_the_Bretton_Woods_Committee>.

## ELEVEN  CREATING A NEW ORGANIZATION

1. Office of the United States Trade Representative, n.d. Web. <http://www.ustr.gov>.

2. Ibid.

3. "Executive Order—National Export Initiative." whitehouse.gov. The White House. Web. <http://www.whitehouse.gov/the-press-office/executive-order-national-export-initiative>.

# INDEX

220          **INDEX**

China—*Continued*
  and entrepreneurialism, 181–3
  and the environment, 128–9
  and exports (U.S.), 27–8
  free trade agreements, 13, 19, 48, 149
  GDP of, 79, 182
  and intellectual property theft, 75–80
  and Korea, 197–8, 200
  market overview, 181–3
  and Opium Wars, 117–19
  population, 4
  and poverty, 182–3
  and the trade deficit (U.S.), 45
  trade policy, 8–10
*China, Inc.*, 77
China Compulsory Certification
  (CCC), 77–8
Choson dynasty (1392–1910), 197
Citigroup, 15
Civil War, 31
Clinton, William Jefferson ("Bill"),
  105, 147–8
Coca-Cola, 137
Cojuangco, Edward, 64–5
Cojuangco Clan (Tarlac province)
  (Philippines), 64
Cold War, 18–19, 101
Colombia, 109–13, 120–5, 148
colonialism, 65–6, 198
Committee on Ways and Means, 76
Communism, 8–9, 26, 55, 100–1,
  106–7, 118, 169, 181, 184, 188–9,
  199–200
Congressional Black Caucus (CBC), 120
Congressional Budget Office (CBO),
  96, 114
Conscientious Equity, 2–3, 5–6, 25,
  30, 38–9, 43, 50, 57, 69–71, 82–3,
  97–8, 101–2, 108, 119–20, 131,
  134, 135–6, 143, 151–3, 164–6,
  171–5, 177–8, 191, 196, 210
  and agricultural subsidies, 97–8
  authority, 151–3
  corruption, 57, 69–71
  definition of, 2–3
  and entrepreneurialism, 39
  and the environment, 131, 174
  and immigration, 135

  and intellectual property, 82–3
  and small business, 171
  as solution, 39, 50
  and trade sanctions, 101–2, 108
  as universal, 177–8
  and voting, 134
  and WTO, 43
Conscientious Equity Accords, 3–6,
  23–4, 38–9, 48, 50, 69–71, 111,
  122–7, 130–1, 133, 149–50, 165
  and the environment, 130–1
  and protections, 124
  provisions of, 5
  and trade, 38–9
consumer economy (U.S.), 4, 135
corruption, 1–3, 5, 38, 56–71, 113, 125,
  171–4, 176
  country rankings, 59
  examples of, 59–68
  and poverty, 57–9
Corruption Perceptions Index (CPI), 59
Cotonou Agreement, 18
counterfeiting, 75–82
Cuba, 100, 104–7, 137
Cultural Revolution (1966–1967), 118
cultures, global, 1–3, 181–210
currency devaluing, 34–6, 113–17

de la Vega, Ralph, 137
debt (U.S.), *see* national debt
Democratic Leadership Council
  (DLC), 120
Democratic National Committee, 145
Democratic party, 120, 122, 145
Democratic People's Republic of Korea
  (DPRK), 199
developing nations, 49, 57–8, 93–6, 105,
  113, 115, 147, 158, 161, 173–4, 200
Diet (Parliament) Building (Tokyo), 183
Dispute Settlement Body (DSB), 47–8
Doha Development Round, 48–9, 96
dollar (U.S.), 34–6, 47, 62, 113–17
  *See also* quantitative easing
Dominican Republic, 20, 70, 125–6
Dudas, Jon W., 81

eBay, 137
Economic Espionage Act (1996), 158